Fallen Acres

A Girl's Voyage Beyond Life Without Her Parents

K.S. Elliott

outskirtspress
DENVER, COLORADO

Fallen Acres
A Girl's Voyage Beyond Life Without Her Parents
All Rights Reserved.
Copyright © 2015 K.S. Elliott
v2.0

Outskirts Press, Inc.
http://www.outskirtspress.com

ISBN: 978-1-4787-5664-4

Outskirts Press and the "OP" logo are trademarks belonging to Outskirts Press, Inc.

PRINTED IN THE UNITED STATES OF AMERICA

Table of Contents

1

Undone

I once saw the World Population Clock broadcasting from a billboard at a casino on I-40 outside of Albuquerque, NM. There are over 7 billion souls taking up space on the planet. While I was watching the clock, ninety-three people died. Sometimes when I go to work, I feel like there are 7 billion people living in my office, or in my head, or in the ladies' restroom. I never find the space I need to be alone. Sometimes I think I'm the only person who feels that way, but I know I'm not. I can't find the room to be alone to hear a song on my headphones. I can't find the space to hear myself think. Because what I've found lately is, since last summer when I first noticed it, I can't seem to get enough air in my lungs to really breathe.

When did that happen? I like to blame it on my history, on where I started. But I used to be able to breathe. When I lived in the house up on the hill, the house that Doug built, I could breathe. The House that Doug built--that's what we called it after Dad had his stroke and lay in the hospital bed. We would tell him his mantra was Rehab-Then-Forty-Acres. The house that Doug built sat on forty acres my parents purchased when they were first married. He couldn't talk and his mind was slow and he was paralyzed on his left side, but we were sure he would go back. He had to go back. We all in one way or another had to go back. There were unfinished pieces to the house-- things we had never done. Some of the undone things were physical, and some of the things just seemed physical, but they were more undone in the heart. Sometimes it can be hard to separate which is which, or when physical undone melts into heart undone.

Like the molding for my bedroom that was still in the garage— the molding that was for the closet Dad built when I was nine, that's physical undone. All the closets looked the same, the built-ins he created, except in his and Mom's room. They never had a closet in their room as long as they lived there. Instead, their clothes were neatly hanging in the hall closets: Dad's clothes were across the hall from the bathroom. Mom's clothes hung in the closet nearest the dining room doorway. The far closet at first belonged to my sister Melanie, but at some point she must have complained and cried, and surely fought with them that she had no place to put her clothes. She shamed them again into thinking they were bad parents. She shamed them into feeling worthless, and downtrodden, the way Mom used to walk after fights with my dad over Melanie, her back bent, her shoulders down, her eyes squeezed into little slits, plodding with the step of an elephant, of someone whose heart feels broken deep inside. That's heart undone, for sure.

I'm sure the homemade closets with the built-in drawers and the top shelf that was always way too high for me to reach was an idea created out of my dad's desire to build. To keep refining things long after the house was done. To have something nicer than the cheap and ugly dressers we might otherwise have had to buy at Kmart, because dressers aren't cheap. My parents had a beautiful solid oak dresser in their room that was in there as long as I lived. As long as they lived--as long as the house was lived in and loved by the people who built it—that dresser was there. That dresser is where my mom hid her jewelry, and where my parents kept their special coins in the blue velvet cloth box that snapped shut hard.

It's where my dad had his handkerchiefs. The ones he shoved down in his back pocket each morning and used all the time until his stroke, when he no longer could wipe his own nose so someone else had to do it for him because he either didn't feel it was dripping or didn't care. He didn't care maybe because of the antidepressants they put him on—because who wouldn't need an antidepressant when you go into a 45-minute surgery to clear out a carotid artery and four hours later you are being wheeled through the basement of a Northern Michigan regional hospital. Past the dark waiting room where your wife and daughter are trying to occupy themselves by changing the ringtones on their phones so they don't see you being wheeled past. Wheeled by the tech that has been told you no longer have use of your left arm, that you can't move it, that all the signs they've seen since you made it to the recovery room mean you have had a stroke. A watershed stroke to be exact, and that your brain tissue is at this very moment dying of suffocation. That no one will know enough or think enough to do anything about it, because it's a small Northern Michigan hospital, because you are an old man, because the surgeon has seen it all before and he is old enough now not to believe anything he does will change the outcome.

That beautiful oak dresser in Mom and Dad's room was not something they could buy for each of us to use in our own rooms, because it was an antique that came from somewhere I'll never know. It was tall, much taller than I was for many of the years I lived at the forty acres in the house on the hill. It was dark wood, but in some places the wood seemed lighter; it had character and depth and it told stories about the person who built it. I imagined it may have come from Woodmoor MI, from someone in my dad's family or his past. Perhaps it was Grandma and Grandpa's dresser. Or maybe one of their seven other children made it with his or her own hands. There were definitely artists in the family. Maybe women weren't woodworkers back then, but they could be artists for sure.

There was my Aunt Eileen who was a painter, and a very, very good painter. Eileen was born a professional artist, for sure, just based on the paintings I have seen. But her paintings were traditional, on canvas, and she made a lot of money from them so she didn't give them away like my Aunt Sis did. Aunt Sis was a different kind of artist. She was not a formal artist, nor was she trained in any way. I doubt anyone even encouraged her painting and from what I remember, she didn't even realize she could paint until she tried it one day in her later years and loved it. After that moment she painted everything and on every type of surface you might imagine. She painted whole landscapes on the inside of a spoon. She painted barns and sunsets on the side of a Popsicle stick. She made murals on bird feathers she glued to stay in place. She could make something beautiful just by making it all over again, from her eye to the stone on which she painted: the feather, the wood, the magnet.

But Aunt Sis was a typical aunt, one who loved her children and grandchildren, nieces and nephews. She was small and round and brown-faced, half Cherokee. She was married to my Uncle Mick, who loved her dearly. They lived next door to my dad's parents up in Woodmoor, a tiny Northern Michigan town. My dad's family pretty much ran the whole town of Woodmoor. Most of the siblings lived on the same road, one right down the street from the next. Aunt Sis and Uncle Mick were easy to love, and they loved each other dearly until my Aunt Sis died in her late 80s. From all visual accounts, it was a simple life they led, easy to admire in its simplicity. The kind of world a child is drawn to for the comfort, like the safe spot in a game of hide-and seek you keep going back to again and again.

Aunt Eileen was a different story. She's a beautiful human being, but she approached the world in a very different way. She's like Jasmine, one of the cats my parents inherited. Two of the cats came from a bad decision I made with a college roommate. After a year we were no longer able to keep the kittens, so they ended up at the forty acres. Jake and Jasmine were their names. Jake was a great cat; he loved to ride in the car. He had amazing concentration. If there was a fly on the ceiling and he spotted it, you could lift him up off the ground and up over your head without him ever taking his eyes off that fly, and he would grab it and eat it. My parents loved that cat; especially my dad. One summer they went on a long camping trip in the motorhome about two years after they inherited Jake, and when they returned Jake was gone. He liked to wander down the road, so they figured someone saw him and opened the car door, and he jumped in, and off he went to live another life with another family.

Jasmine was something else altogether. She was always a little neurotic. Not a very friendly cat, she often stayed out of the way of everyone. That's how she was like my Aunt Eileen. My parents already had a cat when Jake and Jasmine showed up at their house—his name was Tuff. One morning Mom went to the garage to start her car for work and she heard crying, like a baby. After work she heard it still, so she and my dad went in search of the crying sound in the garage. They found a little furry gray kitten that someone must have dropped off near the forty acres and it found its way up to their house and into the garage to the hay and dirty rags in the corner, to the potential for warmth, food, love, and home. They named the kitten Missy, and so she was Missy for about six months until they took her to the vet and found that Missy was a somewhat less appropriate name for her than, say, Mister. So they had Missy fixed, and they started calling her Tuff instead.

Tuff was like my Uncle Ervin. Uncle Ervin was married to Aunt Eileen. He was a ladies' man, so the story goes. Tuff was a nice enough cat, being male and all. He was a little friendlier than your typical cat, but he wasn't so keen on being in a multi-cat household. He liked to throw his weight around. He liked things his way. He wasn't a bully really, but he was all about his own needs and didn't care about the consequences. Things went okay for Jasmine and Jake in the beginning once Tuff got used to them, but after Jake disappeared, Jasmine was alone to fend for herself. My parents always thought that Jasmine was just an unfriendly cat for the first fifteen years until Tuff finally passed away. What they learned was that Tuff was just mean to Jasmine. Not overtly and not in front of them, so they didn't know it was going on. He intimidated her when no one was looking; he made her feel uncomfortable in her own home so she kept quiet. She stayed small and out of the way and that made people believe she was an antisocial cat, not so friendly or nice, when really she was a cat who wanted to blossom but was afraid, was kept down when no one knew.

As soon as Tuff died, Jasmine became a friendly, outgoing, chatty cat who wanted to be part of the conversation and the mealtimes and evening TV hangouts where people had cheese and crackers on plates, or popcorn in a bowl. She wanted to be part of it all. That was exactly how my Aunt Eileen behaved after my Uncle Ervin died.

2

Heavy Hearts of Badness

My dad called all his brothers by their first names, and added the word "brother." Brother Mick, Brother Ervin, Brother Jack. My dad was the youngest of eight children, four boys and four girls. He was the outlier. He struck out on his own, followed his dreams; he never looked back. There was more to this, this way he turned out, than we know—or will ever know. Dad is an introvert who knows his animal, as a pastor once told me. He could talk all the right words in the right places, but it was a cover. I never thought much about who my dad was behind his chatty exterior; there was always something about him that belied a deep well. One recent Saturday night we were facing Daylight Savings Time, so I changed his clocks ahead before I left, knowing then when he awoke Sunday morning he would read the correct time. He insisted Daylight Savings Time was Saturday, and that it had already happened. There was no changing his mind. This was typical of the dad I grew up seeing; once he had decided something, that was his reality. There was no changing it, no matter how wrong he was. His stubbornness was maddening and always had been. Sometimes it was scary, depending on the circumstances. I asked Dad if he was a stubborn Leo—the Zodiac sign. A Virgo, he insisted. We sat down to read that night after his shower and shave, fingernails clean, tucked in beneath six blankets. I found a description of Virgo online. It fit him, perfectly: self-critical, sympathetic, able to read the minds of others in a single bound, but unwilling to share how he felt, even with Kryptonite. How people become brothers, sisters, parents, we know. But who ever really knows any of us?

Eileen was the quiet aunt--aloof, jet black hair, red lipstick. She was never unkind; she just wasn't a kid person. She didn't find crooning to a baby soothing. She didn't want to have a one-sided conversation with a toddler. She had two kids of her own; one I barely knew--a son, and a daughter Luann who seemed to spend a lot of time with my parents in their later years. Luann was in their wedding when she was three; as a young adult, she had been married and divorced with three boys—the twins, and the youngest who got Reye's Syndrome from taking aspirin in the mid-'70s. I always had the feeling Luann caught some judgment for letting that happen to her kid. My mother had compared her to my sister Melanie more than once, perhaps for the way she chose to live her life with what looked like selfishness; after all, how else does a kid get Reye's Syndrome?

Luann took to roaming the country in a motor home before her kids were even grown. Uncle Ervin, from what I overheard in adult conversation, supported Luann in some way or another pretty much up until he died. Aunt Eileen never seemed particularly close to Luann or any of the rest of the family. She didn't participate in the gatherings at Christmastime in the musty township hall at the end of Elliott Road back in the '70s when Grandma Elliott was still alive. Mom never wanted to go either, always dreading having to put on the face and see my dad's huge family when she was an only child and didn't like crowds. I guess she and Aunt Eileen were the outsiders, married in to the Elliott clan and not at all like the rest of them. She fought with my dad about going to see his family. Dad seemed happy to go, but didn't show it much until we got there and he saw everybody. There was something about those years whenever we did go to big family functions, like maybe he felt judged. Or maybe he thought he just wasn't enough.

Whenever there was something going on in Woodmoor, we would make the interminable drive through back country roads. There was no direct way, no freeway exit to get to Woodmoor. You just drove, and turned down road after road until you were there. I would talk to myself on the drive, drawing pictures in the window fog. I talked to myself a lot when I was a kid. My standard playacting was to be interviewed on TV for whatever great thing I had done. The forty acres we lived on were several miles from town, and I didn't have friends over until middle school. I think my mom was too tired to bring other people's children into the house by the time I came along, the last of the three girls--tired from dealing with Melanie, tired from working too much and being anxious all the time. But then I wonder too if she was shielding our family, if my having friends over meant they might witness a fight, or an outburst, or see our family for what it was.

It was better for me if I went outside and wandered alone through the sandy cow pasture to the woods along the perimeter of the property or sat cross-legged in the bathroom sink and stared at myself in the bathroom mirror. When I did this Grace would make fun of me. She would sing the song "You're So Vain." *Why do you always talk to yourself? It's so weird.* I couldn't explain it to her. I felt better when I sat staring into my own face in the mirror or walking alone with my own thoughts spilling out loud from my mouth. I never felt stupid for saying what I felt when I was the only one there, but sharing those things with anyone else would mean ridicule, I was pretty sure of it. I preferred to keep my thoughts and dreams just between me and me.

Our trips up north to the family Christmases went on for years, but I only remember going to them when I was little—little enough that my memories of it are milky, but what's behind the milky-ness is vivid and in motion. I ran around the little township hall with my cousins, wearing a dress with tights, being cold and feeling uncomfortable because I hated dressing up. The memory is like replaying some kind of movie over and over. I wish we had a movie of one of those Christmases, or any Sunday morning in the summer when my parents and Grace and I sat out on the back sun porch for hours. I want to see how we looked and moved and sounded, and remember my parents for who they really were just to make certain my memory is correct. Childhood on the forty acres was a conglomeration of elation and shame; fear of being bad for getting caught being who I was; of hearing my mother say "Stop acting like Melanie." With those words, my mother could shut down any conversation, no matter where it was going.

My sister Melanie was born in 1959, the oldest of the three of us. When it comes to knowing my family for who they are, she might be last on the list. What I know isn't good, and what is good is laden with a big dose of bad—bad memories, bad thoughts, and bad feelings. It seems she was a difficult kid my parents loved, but she didn't love them back. That's the roundabout conclusion I've come to anyway.

From her angle, my dad was mean, my mom was weak, and there was a whole lot of dinner never making it to people's plates, but getting thrown at the walls. The only memories I've stashed away in my brain are from the eyes of a little girl unsure who was right and who was wrong, but who knew all the yelling and throwing could be avoided by either agreeing with everyone, or lying.

Grace is the next oldest; the middle child. Melanie was mean to Grace. Even now Grace hates Melanie and has what I think is a kind of post-traumatic stress for having lived with it all back then. Melanie is what I would call a mean girl. But she's got other problems, and they are the kind a person can't be blamed for. She's pathological in some ways. Who she was then, and how she acted drove a wedge in our world for reasons I didn't understand well and still don't. She left scars on all of us, and my guess is we left scars on her too. At worst, she is reactive, accusatory, irrational, and dramatic; at best she is charming, whip-smart, witty, and fun. A lifetime of reacting to people like this and the situations that come out of it, good or bad, has left a jagged hole in my viscera.

It all started like this: I was about three years old. I think it was winter, or was at least cold outside, because Dad wasn't home. He was up north in Woodmoor hunting with his brothers. I was sleeping. Grace came into my room, crying. She would have been around eight years old. She told me Melanie and Mom were fighting. I handed her the only important possession I had back then—one of two baby blankets I carried with me and later kept under the covers of my bed until well into high school. Grace and I snuck into the dining room where we could see my mom sitting in the La-Z-Boy. Melanie was standing in the living room entryway. I remember nothing about the conversation they were having. I can envision Melanie's biting words coming so fast from her mouth they seemed almost sped up in time; I could see the spit flying from her lips.

The La-Z-Boy was orange, with woven fabric and wooden armrests. Mom was reclined, feet up on the extended foot rest, looking calm and serious. She was not smiling or yelling or hysterical. She was imploring Melanie to understand why she was doing what she was doing, why she was saying what she was saying. Grace and I crouched together—Grace was tiny for her age. I always thought it was because she got kidney infections and was sick a lot, but now I think it's probably just the way she was. Melanie always seemed tall to me because she was nearly thirteen when I was born. She was a teenager then, sixteen or seventeen years old. Mom was scared but she held it all together, I thought, and when I was big, that's how I wanted to handle a crisis. But for now what I knew more than anything was I never wanted Mom to look at me the way she was looking at Melanie just then; I never wanted to feel the desperation I felt, the feeling of words coming out that can never be taken back, the raw emotion of scorching another person.

I would do anything it took to avoid it, which meant keeping opinions inside, because opinions cause conflict and people get angry and faces end up looking like the faces I was looking at right then. Opinions can make people scared, like the little girls crouched on the floor holding each other, watching. Opinions left baby sisters no choice but to protect those who were being scared. Being argumentative meant hurting people and creating an even bigger abyss between yourself and those outside of you. It was much better to agree with everyone, or to just lie about it all, and go find your way without asking questions, or permission. Life was better lived alone than with anyone who would be honest with you, especially if that honesty meant a level of truth that caused pain. It seemed much simpler to never disagree or ask for what you wanted. At the first sign of trouble, back down and take whatever you could get. Then find your way to freedom later. Find your way to what you wanted anyway, whatever that meant.

I don't remember anything about how that evening ended. My vaguest recollections tell me my mom saw us crouching on the floor and would have stopped the discussion, fight over. I would have felt wrong for watching, and bad for getting out of bed, and upset by the scene, but I would haven't said anything. I think Melanie held a knife in her hand that she was waiving as a means of punctuating her words. Maybe she was cutting up a tomato for a sandwich when it all started. But at the time and even now I wonder if my memory serves true--if Mom was afraid of that knife. Then, and even now, I hold this thought that Melanie is villainous; that is what she is in my memory, for so much of it. So much of those years seem long in the past, so long ago we should be able to forget, to forgive and to move on. After all, she was whip-smart, charming and fun too, on the other side of herself. There was an unspoken opinion in me I couldn't explain or ever, ever reveal: somehow I admired Melanie, and I wanted to be just like her.

You might imagine Melanie played a big role in scripting how our family interacted. She certainly scripted how I remember my early life. One day I looked out my bedroom window the summer of my eighteenth year, getting ready to leave for college. I felt that feeling I have when I don't quite know why I feel bad, or what it is I did wrong, but it lays on my heart anyway. Sometime in my thirties I learned to step back from that feeling whenever I got it, to see if it was legitimate, or if it's me doing what my mom always did—the thing Dad told her over and over not to do—worrying about things that haven't even happened. The heavy heart of badness is a trait I think may be part of all five of us—not just my sisters. I think my mom had a heavy heart of badness too, given to her by her mother. I think my dad felt the heavy heart of badness because he didn't want to stay and teach in Woodmoor so he left for Detroit when he was eighteen, stubborn and angry, dropped off on the street by his father and brother to survive on his own.

My sister Melanie feels the heavy heart of badness too, I think, even though we always blamed her for how the rest of us felt. Her way, and Grace's way, of dealing with the heavy heart of badness was always different from mine. Melanie got angry and lost patience and talked fast and made everyone feel nervous and uncomfortable that she was going to blow up and confront us all, making us feel shameful and angry and bringing our heavy hearts of badness right up to the surface where we couldn't squish them back down until she was gone--and sometimes not even then. I believed until my dad had his stroke and my parents moved to Ann Arbor, and we were tasked with being there for them in ways we hadn't anticipated, that my sister Grace was a kind-hearted, soft-spoken soul who loved cats and was a bit shy. Her second husband, Alex, once told me in confidence that in an argument Grace didn't think she was getting her point across unless she was throwing things. I didn't like Alex when they first met and got married, so I surely didn't take his comments as gospel. I thought he was just playing the Baptist card--the card he was born with clenched in his hand, and wanted me to hear about things in his marriage with my sister that I didn't need to hear. But after Dad had his stroke and all of our hearts were beyond heavy, and instead were completely broken in two--maybe never to be fixed again, maybe never to be light and joyful again as long as we lived, I learned things about my sister that changed the way I thought of her forever.

My mom and I were driving one afternoon after she had spent a long day at the hospital sitting with my dad. Grace had made her way home to Canton, and called us. My mom and I were out washing her car and picking up food for dinner. I had just taken Samantha, my parents' furry old dog who was the color of chocolate and looked like a mix between a Shih Tzu and a Cocker Spaniel, to the vet to see an acupuncturist for her arthritis, or what we thought was arthritis, anyway. She was having some pain in her leg and I knew acupuncture had helped Cerin, my Doberman, when he had arthritic feet a few years earlier. As it turned out, Samantha didn't take to acupuncture very well, but it was worth a try.

Mom and I were driving through the car wash when Grace's call came through to Mom's cell. She asked Mom about a procedure the doctor wanted to try on my dad that might help gain some movement back in his left arm. The procedure involved a series of Botox shots that we had tried once already, but the doctor wanted to try again. My mom was hesitant, since it was now eight months post stroke and he could barely talk, could not yet eat solid food, grew angry when the TV was turned on due to the overstimulation, and refused to look at himself in the mirror. Grace asked my mom why she didn't want to do it, getting defensive already. Mom said she would think about it. My sister turned angry, yelling and irrational—saying she didn't understand why Mom would spend money to get the dog acupuncture but not get Dad a second round of Botox treatments.

I felt a fire rush through me when my sister started to yell. It was the heat of shock that my sister was angry and the heat of defensiveness that she would yell at another broken-hearted member of our world. It was the heat of fear at wanting to yell back but being afraid, and the heat of shame for feeling afraid. I didn't confront my sister, and my mom only told her to calm down and go home and relax. My mom took the brunt of her anger and she let it go through her. Because she had learned more quickly than I had something I would soon learn too: no anger that anyone had, no words anyone could throw at the wall would stick to make any kind of difference, because she and I had walked into that hospital room on June 25th and we had seen him; we had seen what we could only comprehend as him staring up at the TV that was in the corner of the ceiling. We had looked at him lying on his back with his head cocked up to the right and we could only imagine he was bored because he had been lying there all night and though they had told us when we left he might not have use of his left arm, we had believed this loss would be what we had to work through with him. He had been depressed for a long time about his aging and his inability to hold his bladder after prostate cancer and surgery a few years earlier, but those things were all pretty normal; things that happen to men in their 70s; people in his generation. After all, Mom had her own tiny messages from her body she chose to ignore until it was too late, but we wouldn't realize that for another two years.

What we knew that morning when we walked into his hospital room after leaving late the night before from the dark waiting room in the basement where the surgeon had come to tell us there was nothing more anyone could do that night; we should go home because he was going home, and we would come back in the morning to assess the damage to his arm. My mom and I had walked toward his hospital room that morning where he faced the door and we watched him for all the steps it took us to get to him from the entrance to the neuro-intensive care unit, to his room. We watched him staring up at the corner where the TV hung, and we believed then that it was his left arm we had lost. We believed it would be years of overcoming that, if at all. We felt afraid of what this might mean and I started thinking of how I would be driving up to my parents' house more often now, since he would be without use of his left arm. There was loss of mobility. We knew that because that's what the surgeon told us. That's what we knew. When mom called his name, Doug, he didn't turn his head. He was stuck. He never turned his head again for several days. He was stuck where his watershed stroke had entered him, brain tissue saturated, dying, unable to let him talk or understand where he was or even control his blood pressure. We realized, with a heavy heart of badness, that we hadn't lost a left arm. We had lost him.

3

Everybody Loses It

It wasn't until much later I realized I didn't have the fear anymore. I used to have a fear, one that seemed to keep hold of me in ways I didn't understand and actually needed some amount of professional therapy to understand. There was first the fear of something happening to my parents. It was nearly an irrational fear and I'm sure it started when I was young. I felt it first when Melanie fought with them, when she screamed and yelled and they cried and my dad grew angry and my mother put my sister Grace and me in the car and drove away, not wanting us to witness what might happen next. I remember the ripping feeling. It was a ripping that left a very long tear in my little child heart, and that tear filled with all kinds of childhood memories of times when my mom trod slowly with her face pinched and her back bent, plodding, sometimes because of my sister Melanie, sometimes because of my dad, and even sometimes because of me. That tear made my heart very heavy with the badness. I was always afraid my parents would leave—they would just grow sick of it all and go. I was afraid they would die from how awful she was, and how much she hurt them. I was afraid, too; afraid to go very far away in case something might happen.

As I grew up, I carried the fear with me. It was a feeling I didn't recognize for a long time. Both of my sisters moved far from my parents. Melanie started her leaving much earlier than Grace did. Melanie first opted to leave as a senior in high school. She was an exchange student in Sweden, leaving in the late summer to spend her senior year of high school abroad. I was four years old. We drove down to the airport in Detroit, all of us. I rode up and down the escalator—something I had never seen before—for what seemed like two hundred times. Another little girl joined me and we played together until I fell on the escalator and my knee bled. On the ride home it was just Grace and Mom and Dad and me. I remember hearing the song on the radio, "Leaving on a Jet Plane," and crying. My sister and parents, with their thinly veiled relief she was gone, were disgusted at my crying. My mother's hair had grown thin from stress and our family doctor had given her a prescription for Valium, the drug of choice in 1975 to help anxious women relax. I didn't know what anyone else was feeling in the car that day. But every time after that when I heard the song, "Leaving on a Jet Plane," I would cry and Grace finally grew tired of it, telling me to stop crying about Melanie. Sometimes she would taunt me and play the song, knowing it would make me cry, and then laugh. Laugh because I didn't get it, but everyone else did.

But I think I was the only one who did get it. What I saw were my parents with their heavy hearts of badness weighing them down with every routine day they lived. I didn't know what they felt, but I knew it must be something akin to feeling like death--like you wanted to die from the guilt, the pain, the regret. I thought of my sister in Sweden, and wondered how she felt. I tried to think of what it might be, but I couldn't guess she felt the way I would have—lonely and alone and questioning my decision, and unsure what to do. Perhaps Melanie and I are the same in this way—maybe we are just a little bit like my dad—we learned to run away and be free and alone and find solace from our heavy hearts in the quiet that comes with having no one, no one really waiting or caring when you came home.

I didn't really experience what it was to leave until I finally did it. I first thought about leaving in high school when maybe all kids think of leaving. My best friend Kara and I talked about California, which only seemed natural. When I was in college I would go to the bookstore section with all the materials on schools in other states. I would pore through them, looking for schools out West. What I wanted, and what I had been looking for since the moment I left the house on the hill, the forty acres, was the feeling it gave me when I returned. I wanted a place that gave me the peace I felt when I wandered the back meadows and the safety I felt when I sat in the tall summer wheat. I wanted a place I could walk barefoot out the door, and talk to no one because no one was there.

4

Mother's Day

I always worried about giving one parent more love than the other. I was afraid of showing favoritism. I was afraid of one parent feeling lonely. I wanted everyone to feel loved. I used to ride with one parent to a restaurant and then ride home with the other so neither of them felt sad at having no one there with them on the way home. Now I suspect my parents would have enjoyed a little peace and quiet on the way home after dinner, to work through their own thoughts. I wonder now if they laughed about that, wondering which one would get a moment of peace on the way home. Talking to my dad now, sitting in his wheelchair wondering things in his mind I can't see or hear or get out of him, because he can't get them out either, he tells me I was "a nice little girl; good little girl." I was, mostly because I didn't want to cause trouble and because I was a genuinely hopeful child. Sunny thoughts ruled my every day right up until I was about eleven years old.

Then one day it changed, and pre-teen hormones started to take over, and suddenly for what seemed an inexplicable reason, I was sad. I felt less than sunny. My heavy heart of badness grew to be more than something that passed with a tangible moment or experience. I felt sad and uneasy; I didn't know why. For a while I spent time trying to find my way back to the light heart I had for the first ten years of life, but that person seemed to disappear. I wanted her back. I thought about her through my high school years, and when all the other stuff went wrong—when the Mother's Day that changed everything came and went, I stopped looking for that girl, because I knew she was gone forever. But still, still, I held on to finding the peace I had on the forty acres. There were some ways I found it, and other ways I grew to find other peace, but those stories are coming. First we have to know what changed everything.

I was in the ninth grade when I met Shane. He was older than me, but he had been held back in Kentucky where his family came from. His dad was an engineer for Marathon Oil and they sent his family to West Pine to live, to drill the wells and find the oil and project manage everything until the people of West Pine were a little richer--at least those who had oil on their properties. My parents had mineral rights, and they were approached by Marathon Oil more than once. For most of their lives my parents resisted, and we never had an oil well on the forty acres. There was never a reason to need it. We had our cows and our garden and our winters and summers on our own little paradise, and we weren't going to ruin it with smells or the continuous sound of wells pounding like two cement blocks smacking into each other over and over and over again. But lots of other people in West Pine did, and the Suarez family was well known in our county.

Shane's dad was an average Latino male, born and raised in the

US. Shane's mother was blonde, grew up in Kentucky, and had gone through gastric bypass surgery several years before they moved to West Pine. She was a large woman: a very large, pale-skinned woman who even after the surgery must have weighed over 300 pounds. She was very nice, and not unattractive, but it was hard to tell what she might have been without the extra weight. Shane loved her to nearly desperation. She was always nice to us, his friends, but I sensed she didn't care for me or trust any other girl around her son. It was my first foray into the theory that mothers who have only boys become so focused on the lives of their boys they somehow forget what it was like to be a girl.

I think what bothered me most about Shane's mom was feeling like she didn't really know me, so it wasn't fair that she was suspicious of me. I had never known people who questioned my worthiness. As weird as my family was, I never felt disrespected or thought of as cheap. Maybe that's part of what made me want Shane to like me even more--it's what allowed me to let him do the things he did. But Shane was a good lesson for me. Because he ruined so many things for me, because he pushed things to a place that was worse than I ever thought things could be at the age of fourteen, he actually gave me something I have held on to since then—an unwavering sense of self-preservation. I should have thanked him for that.

It was the day before Mother's Day, 1985. Shane and I were talking on the phone and he told me his parents were going to be gone that weekend visiting family in Kentucky. He wanted me to come over. I couldn't drive yet and I didn't think my parents would be up for it, but of course they trusted me, looking back. I asked my sister if she would be willing to drop me off at his house. She was still living at home then, going to college but not sure what she wanted to study, fighting with my parents about her future. Mom and Dad didn't want her living at home. Back then things weren't like they are now, when some kids can grow up, go to college, flunk out or graduate, spend a semester abroad, and still end up at home, living with their parents who will work until they die to take care of their kids who never amount to anything. My sister was on a path she couldn't articulate. She was indecisive. My mom hated it. They fought. Grace had always been good at saving money, but she wasn't good at going for it—no matter what it was. I was the one who went for it. I was the risk-taker. I was terrible at saving money, but my life never lacked adventure.

So Shane asked me to come over, and I begged my sister to take me there the next day around noon--just for an hour or two, and then pick me up at the Dairy Queen, which was at the end of town about two miles from Shane's house down a rural freeway. I must have told some kind of lie to someone to get them to do this for me. I lied a lot when I was a kid; that started early and I think it was mostly a way to stay out of trouble—to not get yelled at. To not be told I was "acting like Melanie." I wanted my parents to always be happy with me, but I was a risk-taker and a wanderer and I needed adventure, and adventure almost always meant doing things I shouldn't, which resulted in having to lie to get away with it. Back then I lied and felt bad about it—I always knew it was the wrong thing to do. My badness was heavy a lot of the time.

Melanie came home from college at one point—or at least came home to visit in her twenties when I would have still been a child, and she asked my parents about my lying. She thought it seemed like a problem—which clearly means I was fooling no one. She thought my parents should have it checked out. But they didn't. They were suspicious of her suggestions, always dramatic and jumping to conclusions. They didn't trust her and I always thought it was because she didn't bring it with her into the house, that's why. They would have treated her the way she wanted if she would have given them the reasons they needed, but she always had to make it hard for them. For my sister, confronting them with her truths was the way she felt most authentic, even if it meant she had no relationship with them. For me, conforming was the way I felt most authentic, and it's how I was with my parents. I don't know who was right.

Grace agreed to drop me off at Shane's. On the drive over we talked about Mother's Day dinner and what we were getting Mom. The day was warm and sunny and felt special. I was nervous about going to his house. I wore brand-new pink sweat pants and a plain white t-shirt. Grace dropped me off at his house in the Georgetown neighborhood, up a muddy driveway with no garage. Their house was a rented white ranch-style house separated by proximity and trees from the other more established Tudors and Cape Cods owned by doctors and lawyers in town. They didn't fit in; the minority family from a southern town situated in a house rented for them by Marathon Oil; fish out of water. At some point they moved closer to the oil drills near the West Pine airport, a flat straight road that cut through the middle of the state. I knocked on the door. Shane answered. His brother Tim was on the phone with a friend making plans for the night. The house had a large picture window that looked out over Clayton's house down the hill. The inside was decorated in warm shades that reminded me of the South, where the weather was less severe and people smiled more because there weren't as many reasons to feel cold and isolated and depressed. But it was spring here now too, Mother's Day, and I was at Shane's house alone with him for an hour or so.

5

Careen, As in Off the Road

I think there are people in the world who have a sixth sense, and there are people in the world who do not. This sixth sense is not just about street smarts, or a feeling had just before an event takes place. I'm talking about the kind of sixth sense that gives you pause, even as a child, and makes you realize things long before other people have. When I was nine I realized I never wanted to get married or have kids. I still played childish games of marriage and love; still talked with my friends about who we might marry from our high school someday. Still bought children's books like *The Bad Child's Book of Beasts*, and even wrote in it when I was starting college, "To my firstborn; may you grow up to have only the good monsters in your head." But my sixth sense had already spoken to me and it had told me without a doubt I was destined for things other than marriage and children. This sixth sense isn't born of some kind of uber intelligence; it's not me trying to say those who have it are smarter than others or wiser or better in any way. Sixth sense, as I see it, is simply the realization that we have a path to follow in life, each of us, and learning early on that the closer we try to stay to this path, even when it's inconvenient or hard to do, the easier everything will be. I've learned this lesson over and over in my lifetime, and each time I careen back on to my path after lunging head first into whatever briar patch or deep gully lay to the left or right, I am reminded of the point at which I could have chosen better, I could have saved myself the pain.

Sixth sense is different from making poor decisions. It's interesting how as children and young adults we make poor decisions that affect us so much at the time, but later become just history, just part of who we are. This is what happened with Shane, with the Mother's Day trip to his house, with the little white lies that got me there, and how it changed who I was forever.

So I left off my story with me sitting in his living room. I don't remember much about what we did; probably watched some TV. Looking back, I'm sure Shane and his brother had already talked about all of this. How interesting that Shane and his brother were conspiring to commit things teenage boys should never even think of committing, while my sister and I were planning my drop-off at Shane's house. Our aspirations were different; my sins were never meant to be harmful. My sister wanted to make me happy, and beyond that she was innocent. She would never know what her simple desire to make me happy resulted in. My childish wish to be wanted and loved, to experience something and spend time with my crush was not wrong, but it was fraught with departure from what was right—and still, that's part of being young. These moments become the moments that can take a life in many directions—with the right boy, it might have resulted in memories that brought us to write poems to each other on our birthdays, even decades later, without our spouses knowing about it. We might have sent them to the secret e-mail addresses we created just so we could get birthday e-mails from each other and our significant others would never know. With boys like Shane, these youth-driven events result in the girl becoming a statistic, someone who falls into some unwanted situation that changes her identity, her understanding of herself, forever.

Shane and I watched TV. We didn't eat anything, because I doubt he would have thought to offer me anything. Tim disappeared at some point, either to a neighbor's house or with a girl of his own. Shane and I ended up in his room. My sixth sense was telling me this was a bad idea—but I was also fourteen. I had a heavy heart of badness already. It was hard to be the person who said no at this point. I didn't want a conflict. I went to his room and we were kissing— something I had learned to do the summer after my eighth-grade year with a boy named Rob who was at Alma College for the expository writing course, same as me. We, along with a few hundred other Michigan eighth graders, had taken the SATs as a test group for a study run by the state. They wanted to see if eighth graders could score higher on the SAT than the average senior in high school, and we did. The higher we scored, the more money we got for a scholarship. With my money I took a writing class for two weeks, along with a friend of mine. We bunked at Alma College and I met Rob, who I kissed, and though it seemed unpleasant at the time, I knew I would kiss someone again. He had a broken arm, and long hair. He wasn't much taller than I was. We talked a couple of times after the camp was over, but he lived an hour or so away from me, and soon we lost touch in the way people lose touch with those who have short-term meaning in their lives.

But Shane, who had me in his bedroom and was trying to get me to do more things than my sixth sense said I should, was making me uncomfortable. I wanted him to get off me; we were lying on his bed and he was trying to take off my pants. He wanted to do more. I let it go a little further than I should have. But I didn't let him get where he wanted. Still, he made me lie there until he was done, so I stopped struggling finally, figuring it would be over sooner that way. I hated him, though--I realized I hated him; I hated being forced to do something I asked to have end. I hated that he didn't respect me in the way my family had always done in their own strange way. I hated that he had gotten his parts that close to my parts, because they were mine, and my body is a temple. He broke into my temple and he ruined it.

When he was done, he got off me and I went into the bathroom. I took a washcloth off the towel rack and wiped what he had left on me onto the washcloth. Out of anger and revenge and youth, I hung the washcloth back on the rack. I hoped his entire family would use it to wash their faces, to clean themselves, to rub what he had done to me into their pores.

I walked back to the living room. Tim and Shane were both sitting on the couch. "I need a ride to the Dairy Queen," I told them.

They both sat there, not looking at me. Tim spoke up. "We don't have a car to take you."

Shane looked up in agreement, in support of whatever his brother told me. His eyes told me I was a slut. I was garbage to them now. The girl from a good family, the sweet girl whose teachers loved her, the girl who wandered barefoot on the forty acres, dogs in tow; the girl who was friends with all the other good girls was trash to the boys from Kentucky. These spoiled Kentucky boys, with the mother who indulged them and a father who stayed out of it, had just made a concerted effort to create a situation where they could foul the nice girl, the sweet girl, in her own town, on her turf. And she let it happen. She left behind her sixth sense that had been protecting her since she was three and Melanie waived a knife at her mother, and she let these dirty boys from Kentucky do the worst thing they could do—add even more heaviness to her heart of badness.

I didn't say anything else. I just walked out. Shane came to the yard as I was walking away. He said something like, "See you tomorrow," probably.

Just like that, as I left his driveway and began my two-mile trek down the side of the rural freeway, I changed. I moved to a place in life I had never been before. I was now someone who had been forced into sexual activity by a boy, and then left to walk like some kind of throw-away person down the side of the freeway. I thought this is what it must be like to be homeless, or a prostitute. I got a sense for what it feels like to be shunned after getting pulled into a bad situation and not doing what it takes to get back on the path--not careening back from the briar patch, but getting dragged into the pickers until you are bleeding, and then finally, finally pulling out, so to speak, and clawing back to the road. I think I may have run a little bit in an effort not to be late to the Dairy Queen where my mom was picking me up. The Dairy Queen was a safe zone. It was the place where I could be the girl I had been that morning when I woke up. It was where I could try to claw my way back to the path. I cried and walked; I knew that girl was gone.

6

Those Who Knew; Those Who Didn't

The incident with Shane changed a lot about how I saw myself. It changed the girl I was. I felt outside who I had been. I felt like I had done the ultimate sin of badness. I thought if my parents found out it would change the way they looked at me. I knew they would be mad and upset and hurt and they would question what I had done. They would know I was not the kid they thought I was, or wanted me to be, or I pretended to be. The way I felt about what had happened and how people would react, looking back now, is how the voice in my head taught me to think. It's like how the knife-wielding incident with Melanie taught me to hear the decisions I needed to make from my gut, not my head. It's how I learned to see my future and the path I was on. But this incident in many ways drove the idea of the path into me—made it more visible. Made it something I suddenly understood like I had not before. I carried on my sleeve the incident with Shane, but I hid it deep inside myself at the same time. People might notice something different, but they wouldn't guess what it was.

I never told anyone except one person, a girl I had met in the fifth grade that had moved up north near the Mackinaw Bridge before we started high school. Kim and I were very close when we were younger, our closeness driven by our creative and sensitive hearts. She was someone with whom I could share my poetry and my writing and my thoughts in a way I couldn't with people who saw me every day. When I wrote the letter to her, I was scared what she would think when she read it. Somehow I knew she would not care; whatever she gave me, it was more accepting and raw than what I thought I would get had I told anyone else. I was certain all the closest people in my life would shun me forever. For some reason, I was fairly certain Kim would take the information and understand, without judgment--and she did.

I had always been a church-going kid because my parents had taken me and Grace since we were little, but I wasn't what I would call a religious kid. I didn't say prayers at mealtime, or even at bedtime with my parents listening in. My church had always been the outdoors. But after the Shane incident, I started to read the little Bible my grandparents had gotten me, the one with my engraved name on it. I started to look in there for passages that would help me to not feel so in despair, that would help me get through the next time I felt the heavy heart of badness crushing me. I started talking more and spending time with my friend Elizabeth, who I had met at a wedding completely outside of school when we were about eight or nine years old. I think it may have been the summer going into third or fourth grade. It was Matt Harsh's wedding. He was Melanie's best friend in high school, and the youngest brother of Joyce Harsh Michaels, married to Jim Michaels. They had three daughters: Elizabeth, Jillian, and Denise. It was not unusual for me to have friends in school whose parents had my father for a teacher. This was one of those cases.

The Harshes had gone to school in West Pine, the whole family, and so had Jim Michaels. They married after high school when they were both nineteen. The Michaels were Baptist and went to church at least once a week, sometimes more. They were very accepting of me and they loved me; they treated me like one of their own. I felt like a fraud in their family most of the time. I was not good enough in general, and with my heart of badness I was only tainting the beautiful purity of their family. I loved their house. Jim was a builder and had created the most amazing space at the back of their house—stairs going up to a lofty area where he and Joyce had a bedroom, along with a TV and couch area where the family often piled together to watch Monty Python movies. Huge windows overlooked the forest outside and it felt like being in the jungle. Take the downstairs direction and you ended up in Jim's office and another little space I don't remember much. I felt like the beauty of their home portrayed what was inside them as a family—purity and peace and warmth and truth.

My dad had built our house. He wasn't a builder. He was a man who inside of himself desperately wanted to make something he could call his own. He wanted to find the thing that would bind him to the earth and would be his, that would give him the legitimacy and the honor that came with making something with your own hands, even when everyone else in his family didn't believe he could. So he did. He clawed and worked and scraped. It wasn't the elegant beauty of the Michaels' household, built quietly with time and efficiency. It was digging and scraping and measuring, his brain working and working while is body sweated and he cursed, he got it wrong, he did it over again. It was the difference between how I did things in my life and how others did them. I must have gotten that from him.

The biggest lesson I got from the Shane situation is that I am stronger alone. I don't know if that lesson was a good one to learn, or the right one, but it's what I got and I held on to it. I nursed it and coddled that belief, feeding it and raising it to be a truth that would never be undone. I came back to it over and over again in my life, and it was always there for me. There are times I still wonder if it's true, because the only time I felt it leave me was when Cerin died. I wonder if it will be there when my dad dies; it was there for me when my mom did, but then I knew she would always be with me in some way. Still, the knowledge that even when surrounded by people and situations I could walk away, I could open up the office drawer where I kept my purse, walk out the door and never look back, and I would be fine.

That's what my coworker told me. My crazy coworker, Anne, the social worker with the short white hair who shared an office with me in Flagstaff, the one who accused me of third-party sexual harassment because I told my boss his sweater was nice. That accusation was something I figured I deserved. After all, I was the girl who had to walk down the freeway to the Dairy Queen in her rumpled pink sweatpants. The girl who didn't deserve a ride, the girl who hid her secrets…secrets no one else could understand except for Kim. Kim was a girl who had beautiful curly light brown hair and was cute, so very cute—but she knew it somehow, which only must mean she was a bad girl too. The kind of girl who would understand me when I told her the story of Shane, because after all she was a girl with stories too, with a reputation; I didn't know if any of it was true, but it didn't matter. She was a girl with a heavy heart of badness, just like me.

I never told Elizabeth about the situation with Shane. I never told anyone but Kim and, when I was forty-two, I told Amie, one of my three oldest friends, knowing she would have heard something about me back in high school and would tell me what the rumors were, if they were as big and round and wide as I felt like they were when I was fifteen. Amie reacted the way any 42-year-old grown woman would react to her friend telling her this. She may have reacted the same way at fifteen. But I'll never know.

Elizabeth and I shared many secrets. We talked about lots of things beyond boys and school and worries. We talked about the future and we talked about God. We read books in her room that had the adjoining bathroom so I could talk to her while she sat on the toilet. We didn't do that in our family, but in her family, they did. We slept on the floor in her room--or I slept on the floor anyway, on couch cushions. I didn't like sleeping that way; it was uncomfortable and I felt like people are supposed to sleep in beds. Friends should have beds for their guests to sleep in. I had an extra bed in my room for my friends. My outer world was smiles and happiness, but my inner world insisted on routine, things I understood, the standards, what was appropriate. It was why I was better alone.

Elizabeth and I made cookies and we went to church. Her mother would call the girls in one long sweeping voice—LizzyJillyDeni--when she wanted them. It was easier than remembering which girl she wanted. Elizabeth's mother, Joyce, was sweet and laughed often. Elizabeth's family was smart, and charming, and loving. Jillian was the quiet one. Denise was the youngest—pouty, obstinate. She struck me as the one who would break out and do the wrong things. I don't think she did. I think they all turned out to be loving parents who still spend holidays and time together, lots of time. They still go to church; they are still a better people together than they are apart.

7

Who They Were

My sister Grace and I often texted back and forth about problems with Dad once Mom was gone and his well-being fell completely to us. We didn't spend much time together as adults. Since she moved out of the house after her first marriage, we saw each other once a year, and for the most part I found her kind of annoying. We were very different people driven by different things who dealt with life in very different ways. But Grace was still my big sister, and had been there for me through a lot of good and bad times with Melanie and my parents. She taught me to tie my shoes, to ride a bike; we used to skip arm-in-arm down the driveway singing "We are buddies." She was the same little girl who came to my bed late at night when I was three, upset and crying because Melanie was standing in the dark entryway to the living room on the yellow linoleum floor my mom picked out because she loved the color yellow so much, and wielding a knife--a knife that for the life of me when I thought about it again, I could not remember. Was it a sharp knife? Was it the one with the oak handle my grandfather made when he was in WWII? Or was it more like a paring knife, the kind of knife she would use when she was peeling an apple, and then happened to get into a heated discussion with Mom, and walked to the shadowy entryway between the dining room and the living room, leaning defensively against the door, but really she didn't mean any harm.

Maybe she never meant any harm. Maybe she was just sad and confused and wanted love but didn't know how to ask for it, like Mom and Dad didn't know how. Like Dad's family took him, their diamond-in-the-rough, to downtown Detroit when he was eighteen, and left him there to drop his books getting off the streetcar. It was an act of love, but it didn't look like it. Maybe Melanie was afraid. Like Mom was afraid to let down her guard, to be free, to be the girl she wanted to be instead of being the good girl, the well-dressed girl who was loved by my grandparents maybe too much, who left behind her dreams to be a doctor when she had the chance in the 1960s because my mom had a family—the girl who never got the things in her life she really wanted, because she didn't really ever let herself know what she wanted. So Mom ended up with a man she mostly loved who mostly loved her back, for fifty-two years. But she never really was who she wanted to be. And maybe he wasn't either. And they had a girl, a little girl, who was all their worst traits and all their hardest parts and all their lost dreams brought out in the open. She made it hard for them to forget that they put away their dreams.

My sister Melanie was a difficult person who I loved and admired; she was also someone I despised and every time I saw her, by the time the visit was over, I didn't ever want to see her again. She was nice to me when she wanted to be, but didn't hide her dismay with me when I was little—when I was just myself. But there was more to it than that. She didn't look out for me like Grace did. She was selfish and self-centered. She was angry and outspoken. She caused pain and discomfort and awkward family moments whenever she was there. When she wasn't there, we all felt our own part of the anxiety that came with what might come if she appeared.

Even into my twenties I was the one who evened out the situation. Anytime she came home for the holidays, bringing along her current boyfriend or strange bedfellow, she would enjoy secretive looks with her guest, as if our provincial ways were amusing and exactly what they had expected based on all she had told him in preparation. We all felt small, but still, there was power there. And yet I think she felt powerless. I think her powerlessness was felt by my parents, who also felt powerless, and by nature a family of powerless people will all handle it a little differently. My sister Melanie fought, my sister Grace yelled, my dad attacked physically, my mom turned emotionally cold; I learned to hate all of these behaviors in life, to avoid them in my own life, no matter what it might take.

When I was twenty-nine I decided, as a New Year resolution, I would spend more time with Melanie and her husband Jed. I made an effort to reach out, invited myself to visit their home in Philly where my parents had driven out several times with their dog, Samantha. The house Melanie and Jed lived in was the old-style Philly row house; it had a third story off the hallway with a door at the bottom of the stairs. My parents went there in their motorhome. Mom called me to say that when she saw the floor they were staying on, with the only exit being the stairway from the second floor, she had a lingering fear Melanie might set the house on fire and leave them in there to die. Or maybe she would come up the stairs and stab them to death.

I stayed in that same room on the third floor when I visited. There were stars on the blue painted slanted ceiling, and a comfy Ikea bed that always seemed more authentic when it was in Melanie's house since she had lived in Sweden for several years. I thought briefly about the fire potential and the fact that I was trapped up there, much like my mom felt. When I visited Melanie she told me that Dad had abused her when she was little. He and Mom yelled and hit her, so she would run away to the swampy area behind their trailer. She feared for Grace when she was born because she worried my dad would hit her too. This information was too much. Too much for me to hear, because I knew when I was little my mom would take Grace and me away in the car when Melanie and my dad fought. I had seen him get physical with Melanie and once with Grace too, putting his hands around their throats when the fight hit its worst. But he had never, ever acted that way toward me. Was he physical because they acted like jerks and deserved it? Does anyone deserve to be grabbed by the throat and reminded who is in charge? Maybe everyone deserves to be grabbed by the back of the neck when they think they are in charge, and are not.

I don't know. It wasn't up to me to decide. I was the kid who never had that happen because I was good—I had a heavy heart of badness just like everyone else in my family, but I never let it get the best of me. I never raised my voice and I felt okay about that. I felt superior to my sisters because my parents never got mad enough at me to grab me by the throat. I prided myself on being the good kid. My parents and I learned to get along like roommates after my sisters were gone; we each had our household duties. I followed the rules. They learned not to grab and yell and throw food when they got mad at each other. I learned to skirt any situation that would put me in a position to meet that kind of anger head-on.

When I returned from Melanie and Jed's house in Philly I told my boss, Bruce, what Melanie and told me. Bruce and I worked together, and we were friends too. He listened and wondered and had the same puzzled questions I had. Perhaps he just felt sympathetic and wanted to support me. Perhaps, like me, he really wondered if my dad was capable of abusing a little kid. I mean teenagers who are snotty might be one thing, but a child? That's different. Maybe he already knew the answer to that question I kept mulling in my head. Bruce could put all the stories together, an objective outsider, and see—yes, of course my dad was capable of it. That's how the heavy hearts of badness started in our family. Mom and Dad did wrong by Melanie when she was young, and they never really worked it out, with her, or with themselves. Then came Grace. By the time I came along I doubt that kind of explosive anger was even my dad anymore. At the very least, by the time I hit my teenage years my parents had worked through enough of their growing up years, their personal frustrations, their disappointments in themselves and each other and the world as a whole to see any reason to grab me by the throat. And I think they knew me well enough to know I was never going to be that kid anyway.

I spent a long time feeling like crap about what I had learned, and then I finally let the thoughts go. I never confronted my parents or told them the secret I had with Melanie. Instead, the whole situation took me to a therapist asking the question, "Why can't I bring myself to go back to Arizona where I want to be?" After several months, she brought me to the conclusion. It was a conclusion that was truthful and real and raw and it made me see things I would never have guessed. I had an epiphany: I was afraid to leave to go to Arizona because I thought my parents didn't like the idea of my leaving, and every time my sisters did something in my life my parents didn't like, my parents rejected them. My whole problem, my whole issue with Arizona and moving west and having my own space was driven by the fear that if I did what I wanted, and went away, my parents would reject me, and that was a death far greater than any real loss I would actually face with my parents, not long after I came back from Arizona for the last time.

Once I figured out the issue, it was simple. My parents wouldn't reject me for going west, for following my dreams, for making my life what I wanted to make of it. For me to think that they would do anything else was completely crazy. I felt free and I made decisions with abandon and I did go west, with the job of my dreams, in a town I thought was amazing, and bought a house I couldn't afford in a neighborhood where drunken locals rested their backs against my fence and threw broken bottles into my tiny back yard, hitting Cerin in the head. There were reasons I went back to Arizona, there were reasons I left again less than two years later, and in the end all if it was part of the plan, the path, and was in so very many ways completely out of my control.

8

Regrets, I Have Them

There were times in my life when I felt very alone. That's not so unusual. Everyone feels alone sometimes. We are alone in our worlds no matter where we are or who we are with. When my mom was actively dying in the American House Independent Living apartment we had rented for her and Dad while she wasted away for the seven weeks she lived after we found out she was sick, I realized something. Mom was sick with something she could have saved herself from had she thought to save herself, but she was afraid of the immediate pain, not what might come next. Mom died of metastatic liver disease. That's liver cancer that has metastasized from somewhere else; in her case, her colon. She had one colonoscopy in her whole life, at age fifty-four. She was allergic to the anesthesia, and it made her violently sick. She nearly choked to death on her own vomit in the hospital after the procedure. So she made a decision to never have another colonoscopy. It wasn't a decision she shared with anyone necessarily, or discussed the consequences of skipping such a procedure, she just did it. Had we all been smarter and thought ahead, had we talked a little more proactively to each other and even to ourselves, there are so many things we could have saved ourselves from, at least for a little longer—Dad's stroke, Mom's liver cancer; our family history. But there are some things that would have happened no matter what, like Cerin dying. And for those things, we have to accept that there is the path, and the plan. No matter how hard we try some things will happen sooner than we want, but with a little help from ourselves, we can steal time, moment by moment.

Cerin was a five-month-old Doberman puppy when I rescued from the pound. He was with me day and night for eight and a half years. The last two years of Cerin's life, I was focused on his dying. By June 2010 when everything about life had changed so dramatically, when everything I had known to be was no longer, I looked back to see what I might have done differently. Funny how that comes to be—life as we know it, with hind sight so vivid it makes us realize what we might have done differently. Life as we didn't want to think it could be sometimes happens anyway, as it should. What I mean by all of that is Cerin died before my parents got sick. And Cerin's death was the beginning of the end for me. It was the first thing I really understood I feared and the anxiety I carried in my heart for more than eight years. That fear of losing him meant a lot of things I couldn't put my finger on: it was his death, my loss of something I couldn't live without, which translated to my parents—two people I didn't know how I would live without. My fear of loss drove it—the fear of facing things head-on in the way I talked about with my therapist before the last trip to Arizona, wasn't something I could really comprehend until it happened. Sometimes the end is really where we begin.

My grandparents had died—my mom's parents—when I was in my twenties. I remember vividly the last time I saw my grandmother getting out of the back seat of my parents' car. They had brought her to their house to die, and as I walked by her for the last time in her life, I didn't even hug her. I didn't support her or hold her close. I walked by her as she was being helped out of the car into my parents' home, to lie in the back bedroom, to be visited by the hospice nurse who taught my mom to give her shots of morphine, just enough to stop her pain but not enough to kill her. Mom was told me she wondered why she shouldn't give my grandmother enough to kill her. Why not? I couldn't say why. I couldn't because I was young and wanted to not think about death, or pain, or something in my heart that meant I had to feel what I couldn't yet feel—or didn't want to feel. When you are little you dream of the people who care for you, and you see them and they hold you and you live to please them, or they live to please you, depending on the kind of child you are and the family you have. I lived to please, but even when I was young, I knew these people couldn't stay with me forever. But them leaving—the act of having them gone—it wasn't something I could do. I ran from that. I ran like most people might run—especially people in their twenties.

Grace's second husband has two girls, all grown up and married, or at least one of them is married. Their mother died several years ago when they were both in their early twenties. Grace tells me the girls were around when their mother died, but they seemed so untouched by it, so insensitive to her death. It's their youthfulness, I tell her. It's their way of handling it. They are invincible and unable to comprehend or feel the death because their warrior hearts, their hardened hearts of badness or whatever they have grown up with inside their chests, cannot take time out at this juncture in life to live less, and grieve more. It's only when our heavy hearts of badness grow older, and wiser, and weaker, but stronger somehow too, are we able to stand in front of the fear we face, our mothers breathing their last breaths, our fathers standing solo with some help in the bathroom of the spaces they now call home, letting us care for them. We see things of theirs we do not want to see, but we see because we are still warriors—but now we are humble warriors, warriors both harder in heart and softer in heart, with souls that mumble at night when we are alone. We are okay with helping our fathers stand solo at the bathroom sink while we help them brush teeth and clean themselves. We are okay, we accept our mothers lying in beds breathing their last breaths, with someone watching over them while we sleep so we can work the next day. We only regret what we have or haven't done once it's over. We only then think we could have done it differently. But it's too late. We can't change it. It's another thing to regret.

Regrets are a part of human life. My world is full of regrets. But my world is a wonder. It's a wonder of the things I have seen and felt all my life. Sometimes my life feels like it runs a course in front of me and I just follow the path until it ends; sometimes I feel like it's almost done. It's almost done already, at forty-three, and if I achieve the last of my life goals I will have done all I needed to do. I'm afraid of what God and the Universe will say to me then. I had a beautiful friend in high school, Rory. She was sweet and faithful, raised Catholic, and by her junior year had reached a point in her faith and good works in life that seemed very tangible to her, real and complete somehow. We talked about it during track practice one day. I was leaving for college in a few months, and we talked about being roommates when she graduated the next year. A week later on my 18th birthday, she was struck by lightning getting off the school bus and died. She had reached a point on her path and it felt good to her. She experienced it, and then she was gone.

When I moved to Arizona the second time, I bought a townhouse. I closed on the property on my 36th birthday. I felt powerful and free. I was alone and I didn't need anyone else to have the things in my life that mattered to me. I had my life and my job; I had overcome my fear of disappointing my parents by going back to Arizona. I was where I wanted to be. I thought I would live there, with Cerin, in my colorful house with the mossy green living room walls, and the red kitchen accents, and the winter pink shade in my Jack and Jill bathrooms until my life was done. I thought these places would stay with me forever and were mine; they were a part of me. Even the black VW Golf I bought in Phoenix on a whim because my green Nissan pickup truck didn't fit in the one-car garage felt like an accomplishment of decisions that took me closer to the penultimate of my existence on Earth.

In the meantime, I tried to live in the moment; I didn't look ahead beyond the grass seed I planted in my back yard around the base of the gigantic pine tree that spilled out into the side yard. I built a tiny fence from the side of the house to the end of the sidewalk as a way of delineating my property from the empty lot next door where the vagrants walked through to get to the park. They would urinate on my garage. They would spray paint graffiti on the side of my house. I called the police regularly after I moved in, filing thirty-six police reports in the first seven days. I desperately ran toward what I thought was progress toward things everyone should have in life—a house, a dog, a car, a job. But I still felt weird. I kept making mistakes and I couldn't figure out why. I kept doing things I regretted.

Within six months I realized the house was too expensive and I couldn't afford it. I borrowed money from people who had trusted me, telling them I would pay them back as soon as possible. I created circles of debt, swimming and drowning and circling more debt. I made bad choices. I brought Cerin to work so the in-house vet could look at the foot he injured during a hike in the mountains. I left him in the car for what was supposed to be a few minutes but turned into a couple of hours, and when I went back out with the vet, I realized it seemed hotter than I thought it was outside and I shouldn't have left him in the car even with the windows down. He was fine but he had defecated on the back seat. Like a guilty parent caught in what is clearly neglect that could have turned into something worse in an instant, but was never intended as anything other than a stupid mistake—I didn't mean for him to be in the hot car so long—but now I see it's hot, and I shouldn't have left him. I was apologetic, falling over myself. My choice was suspect at best, and I could have killed him. "But I love him, I love him," I kept saying to the vet. I didn't mean for any of this to happen.

I had dragged myself back to Arizona, having gotten past the obvious fears. I was unsure then why I wasn't happy. Northern Arizona had felt something like the forty acres; I knew it when I arrived there the first time. But it wasn't. There seemed to me, no matter how hard I looked, I couldn't get it back—that calm in me that came with the forty acres. By now the place it had been was gone, bought by another family after we put it up for sale when Mom died. Everything was gone from that life with the exception of my dad. Even he is a different person than he was on the forty acres. Now I take care of him like I did when I was little and it was summertime, and he would come in the house after having worked outside all day, sweaty and tired. He would lie down on the living room floor and I would sit on his back with a cold washcloth over his neck and scratch the skin on his shoulders and sing him songs. The TV would be playing the news or a mid-afternoon game show, but it didn't matter. I would talk the whole time and he would just lie there, listening. Maybe he just wanted to come in the house after working hard on the house that he built for all those years to find patience and love, unrequited, all-encompassing, non-judgmental acceptance. Sometimes I look into his eyes now, as I shave his face or trim his nails, and he whispers to me in triplicate, everything in triplicate, to tell me it's all right, yup, yup, yup. I think about my life, my regrets, all that I wish I had not done, or done differently, and I think it doesn't matter now; it doesn't matter what I lost back then, because today it's just me, and him, and that's good, good, good.

9

What It's Like

The morning we first went back to St. Mary's and found my dad with his head looking up and off to the side, as if he somehow watched his life escape out the top of his head, my mom and I wondered if he would live. We walked out of the hospital room together, to the nurse's station. A lovely young woman wearing shiny black Danskos came up to us. Her face was sympathetic and soft and it said to us that she understood how hard this must be, but it is what it is. She would be there to support, but she couldn't change anything. It would be up to us to accept, and she would do what she could to help that process along. Her name was Jill. All the nurses at the station who had come on that morning, I discovered later, thought that my mom and I knew Dad's condition when we arrived. They didn't realize the devastation we met when we came into his room. We would go through a lot of that over the next couple of years, the feeling that we were living in a Plexiglas bubble, with everything else going on around us, like some kind of silent treatment.

"You're going to lose your father," Mom said. We walked out of the neuro-intensive care unit into the hallway to the left, quiet and clean and colorless, toward the windows where we would make our first phone calls letting the world know our lives as we knew them had ended. All of us alone in our ending; for my mom it was the beginning of an end she couldn't even comprehend yet. For me, it was the terrifying truth I had avoided so successfully that I now hardly believe it was here. My mom started calling their friends. I can't remember who she called first. She asked me to call Melanie. I dialed; it rang, she picked up, I told the facts. "Okay," she said. "Okay" was the same word I heard from her husband. I wondered, is this how therapists and social workers deal with bad news? She and Jed were both PhDs with social work backgrounds. It seemed wrong, or odd to hear nothing more. All I knew was when I was feeling the stabbing, throbbing, searing pain in my heavy heart of badness, all she could say was "Okay."

After a few phone calls we walked back to my dad's room. It was warm, June 25, and sunny. We were in an unsavory part of Saginaw, and there was nowhere to eat. We had packed a cooler of tiny peanut butter sandwiches cut into fours. I used a technique I saw on the Food Channel: put the whole sandwich into the Ziploc bag and then use a plastic spatula to cut it into fours. No mess. We sat in my dad's room with him, my mom in a chair stationed close by him, me off to the side near her. We listened to the beeping of the monitors. We watched his blood pressure climb and plummet. We talked to the nurses when they came in: Jill, Chris, Mary, Sheila. There was gravity in their tones of voice, respect in the way they walked and dealt with Dad. We listened to each other. We were gentle. We were like tiny blown crystal figurines waiting to be bumped by the dog's tail on his way to the water dish, falling and crashing to the ground, breaking apart with no possible hope of repair.

Grace and her husband were supposed to be at a wedding in Minneapolis June 25. They went anyway, despite the problems we faced, because that was their plan. That was their plan and they had yet to realize that wasn't how life could go anymore. We figured it out immediately, Mom and Scott and I, but it took Grace and Alex longer. They still thought they could save the money they had put away to fix up their basement. It took them a few weeks to realize that money would have to go to pay for multiple trips to Michigan, and finally for a moving truck to bring my sister here semi-permanently--for three years, anyway. They still thought Mom might help pay for their tickets back to Greenshore from Michigan like my parents had done for them in the past. Perhaps I can't blame them. Even Mom hesitated to cancel her and Dad's camping reservations in Nashville for September. And I...I didn't understand Jill when she told me, in no uncertain terms, "He will be whoever he is going to be now." I didn't have the faintest idea what that meant. None of us were able to comprehend how this would change our lives. I can't blame Grace for what I saw as her self-centered short-sightedness.

Much like Melanie, who never came around to see anything beyond herself, Grace sat somewhere in the middle, finally leaving her personal agenda to make the best possible teammate, like a volleyball judge or the kid holding the middle part of the rope in a giant tug-of-war, who gave in to the winning side. She ended up with me, firmly, on my side, but somehow even then I felt alone with my end of the rope, waiting any moment for her to let go entirely, or maybe it was I who worried that I would let go, without warning.

Dad stayed in the neuro-intensive care unit at St. Mary's for four weeks. By the time he moved back home, I could recite the dates Dad was at each facility. St. Mary's: June 24-July 25; St. Joe Select Specialty: July 25-Aug 24; Oak Glen: Aug 24-Nov 26; St Joe Rehab: Nov 26-Jan 11. Just like Dad, I had the gift of remembering dates for odd reasons, dates and times. When we were kids, he could remember dates better than we did, and he was always right. As he grew older he would be off by a day or a week, but didn't like admitting it even before his stroke. He doesn't like being wrong, especially when before he was always right. I never liked knowing my dad was wrong. I liked him being right about things. I never wanted to tell him he was wrong, then or now. Even years after the stroke when he was far less of his old self, and I had been his primary caregiver--I had been the one who was right, almost always--I still hated correcting him. I didn't do it at all unless it made a material difference. What did it matter? Mom was the only one who could argue with him when he was wrong. But it didn't change anything. He was still stubborn and refused to hear it, and she would eventually just let it go.

That's the difference between each of us. My sister Grace would argue back, and so would Melanie. They didn't let it go. They stuck to their guns, right or wrong. I'm not that strong. I don't give someone the chance to tell me I'm wrong, because I just don't show them the passion. It saves me time and emotion. It keeps me from the messiness of correcting my errors. And I have made many errors. I'm just too weak and tired now to fight for the truth. Maybe this actually makes me worse than those who refuse to give in.

For lunch we would go outside on the grass in front of the hospital and eat our peanut butter sandwiches cut into fours. We chewed on our apple slices and we walked the dog. Samantha came with us sometimes and sat in the car. Most days she stayed home and we had the neighbor let her out. She figured out fairly quickly there was a problem, that something had changed. She had been with my parents for fifteen years, so she knew the patterns. She sensed my mom's anxiety and the deepness of her pain. It smelled all over her like a damp summer blanket, like something in cut grass that had gone rank. Slowly the desperation in all of us disappeared and we settled into a depression that felt more like the corners of the pole barn, all cold cement and dead crickets and sand from the boat tires that blew as far to the outer walls as it could go before becoming trapped and forgotten.

We went through all the motions of people who had lives that were humming along normally until the moment everything went off the rails. My parents had bananas sitting in a basket under the little hanging driftwood near the corner of the kitchen counter, purchased the day before the surgery. They grew brown, then rotted. Sometime in the summer we threw them away. We had fun-sized Snickers bars in the cupboard next to the lazy Susan. They developed a white film from the chocolate melting and hardening again. Dad's gloves sat on the floor of his pickup truck, which sat outside the garage for most of the year. We didn't remove those gloves from their spot in the truck; we left them for the estate sale company to deal with. Things sat, as they were, as if time had stopped. I guess it sort of did. For Mom, life turned the corner from good and happy to bereft and empty. Dad went into a limbo state where he would be whoever he was going to be now, as Jill said. I hated that she said that. I didn't understand her. It would be a long time before I could.

10

Everyman

There was a point to all of this madness, we believed, to all of this time we were spending waiting for him to recover, to be the man we remembered him to be. For us to walk into his hospital room and find him sitting at the edge of the bed with his glasses on, holding the plastic bag we had brought to put his effects in, the ones they had given back to us after surgery. We waited patiently, like baby birds, mouths open and eyes shut, certain beyond certainty the worm would drop into our mouths at any moment, and he would be delivered back to us as he was before. Though it was obvious to anyone else this would never happen, we were not ready to know anything differently. Still, there were tell-tale signs we could not ignore. My dad wore glasses his whole life, but now, now the glasses hurt his nose and bothered his vision. He would not have so much as sat up in bed without putting his glasses on for the last seventy years of his life. Now, with one event, his eyes were changed, and the frustration of not being able to see with his glasses made him throw them violently across the room with the one hand he could still use. But we needed him to wear the glasses. The glasses meant he was still who he had been. They meant he was going to be what we remembered, and this was all temporary.

The same was true for his clothes. My mother brought a change of clothes for him the first day: khaki shorts, a t-shirt, white socks. His black belt he always wore. We soon learned this standard attire was a no-no, as he would say. We might as well have chucked the black belt out the window on the way down I-75 from West Pine to Saginaw; he would never need it again for the rest of his life. Still we couldn't comprehend this. The person we knew wore a clean shirt every day and he wore pants, the kind with buttons and zippers. He washed and shaved and was clean and presentable every day of his life. The person we knew did not lie in bed naked from the waist down under hospital sheets, an adult diaper underneath him. He would never allow this. Yesterday he was different. He was the person we knew yesterday. We did not know who this person was.

The feeling I took with me from what happened to my dad could be described as nothing short of a broken heart. My heavy heart of badness broke straight in two, and for a very long time I never believed I would feel anything less than the deepest sadness ever again. I lived in that state of mind, in that bubble of anxiety and pain, and I think it's something people can understand only if they live through an event that brings them that kind of pain. It is a unique pain, the pain of unalterable loss that does not come with another person's death, but instead with their continued existence when death would have been better. This loss accompanies the five stages of grief, but the healing part—the part that eventually gets better after someone dies--is missing. He did not die. He still lived, but he lived now as a person we did not know and with a body and brain he would not want. Looking back, if he had died we would have all suffered less—including him. Still, there have been blessings that came with this half-loss; the rebuilding of a life that is one day strong and the next destroyed. In how many ways could we count ourselves destroyed with him, at first, and for a long time after? In how many ways did my mother feel herself destroyed, her dreams and the world she knew? She could not do anything but let it take her too, eventually, with liver cancer two years later. My friend Kate, who is from Australia, told me one day as I sat in her kitchen that I would not always feel this way. Things would not always be the way they were. Such a simple thing to say, it seemed, but her words were a laser beam of light. Her words said something to me that made a path through the darkest place to somewhere brighter. I wasn't sure I believed her entirely, but really, I wanted to believe her. I wanted it to be true and I knew Kate had been in a similar place at some point in her life. Her brother had died in a car accident in his twenties. She remembered sitting with her father at the hospital. I wondered if she could have felt what I was feeling—if she could understand the raw wound in my stomach. I chose to believe she did.

I had another friend whose father had died after suffering for a while with organ failure. Though I fully expected she would understand how I was feeling, I realized people are not always who we think they are. All this uproar, this emotional upheaval, it makes us think we don't understand our world anymore. It makes us question all the more that things are not as they seem. We lose confidence. Before the stroke, I was a senior analyst for a market research company. I had a master's degree. I worked hard and was respected by my coworkers. My parents were proud of me, but losing people to sickness changes things. I couldn't keep my job; I was too tired to be a professional anymore. I didn't want to read data and analyze information, and write reports with recommendations because I didn't care about the data anymore. I was spending my time hoping my father would cling to the edge of his life one more day. I saw everything differently now. I saw everyone as the average man. Everyone I looked at in my mind would someday be old and lie in a bed barely covered by a sheet leaving all manner of excretions soaking into a diaper underneath. Every single person had an impending history I thought I knew. I thought I could predict it for everyone now, because I had seen the worst and was making my way through it. I didn't care anymore what people thought. It didn't matter what I said or how it was taken. Because my dad had a stroke, and he was no longer who I thought he was, and the world I had come to know on the forty acres with lilacs and birch trees and budding tiger lilies that ran along the deck was dead to me, dead to him. Nothing else mattered.

There were a lot of people I thought would understand what was happening to us, but who didn't. There were others who never seemed to grasp the gravity of the situation, even if they had been there at some point. My friend Kara came to visit my dad. She had known my parents since she was in elementary school with me. My oldest and dearest friend, she openly cried when I walked her back down the hallway to the waiting room at St. Joe. Kara had my dad as a teacher in high school, and so had her parents when Dad first started teaching. That happened more than once. My parents had me during their later years. Many of my friends were the oldest or nearly the oldest in their families. The generations crossed, which made for interesting stories.

I had friends who felt betrayed at times by the frequency with which my parents took precedence over things I had planned with them. There was no more planning for fun. Dealing with this situation with my parents was my plan. And when I had friends who reacted differently than I did to their own parents' declining health, it was always a shock. My friend Alicia's father was sick and in the hospital—he's the one who had the organ failures. She laughed one day when she recalled how he had swollen up from all the fluids they pumped into him. Like the Michelin Man, she said. My dad did not swell, but his neuro-intensive care unit nurse Jill had prepared us for that. My heart felt like it was made of paper all the time. When Alicia could laugh about this, about her dad swollen and odd, I couldn't understand—it was as if she spoke some language I didn't know. It was as if she were the mean girl in school making fun of the boy stuttering in class. It was just her way of dealing with her own situation. There's nothing wrong with that. But for me, it was the cruelest manner of laughing. It was unknowable to me.

For four years after my father's stroke and my mother's death I cried for things I never would have cried for before. They weren't things that didn't warrant crying over, but I had always prided myself on being able to work through the moment when I was almost brought to tears. I felt in control when I could imagine the colors of shoes lining my closet during the saddest part of a movie. While everyone else let go, I could still hold it together. My mom was strong that way; she never cried at her own mother's funeral. She kept her grace. She never wavered in the face of Melanie's irrational anger. She could scoff back at my dad when his teasing turned mean. I took pride in being like that too. But after she died, and he changed forever, all sense of holding it together was torn away. I didn't have what it took to hold it together anymore. After a while, it didn't matter. I cried when my friend Lilly came back to work from Thanksgiving weekend having been in a car accident with her sister. She was sore but otherwise fine. Before all of this other stuff, I would have been shocked with her at what happened and horrified at how awful it must have been. But now I pulled her hands to me and cried. I cried at the fear she must have felt. I cried because she could be dead. I cried because her sister took her attention off the road for a minute and felt guilt for what could have been. I cried for how all of our lives would have changed. How could I not have always cried at this? I began to wonder.

11

Location, Location, Location

The first battle Mom and I had to fight to protect my dad was not at all what I would have guessed it would be. It was to keep him from being kicked out of St. Mary's. When someone you love lies dying in a bed, if they lay there long enough, there comes a point where the hospital decides to fill the bed with someone else. I'm not sure what the formula is, but I'm quite certain it's driven by money, insurance, and profits. Because much like in my early college years when I thought I might want to become a vet, when I actually did get a job working for one I discovered it becomes like a business. A love of animals is important, but for reasons of necessity, it becomes secondary. The business of caring for humans is no different. The formula for human value is not for me to decide. But it was of the utmost importance to the discharge planner. My mom saw this coming since she worked in hospitals and nursing homes for most of her career in one aspect of administration or another. I never did ask her, though, because when it is your sick person who lies in the bed, you don't care to talk about the rationale for kicking them out. You want them to either come home to you, or go to the best possible next option. St. Mary's wanted my dad to leave the next day, and with a tracheostomy sticking out of his throat, he wasn't going anywhere we would pick for him, and most definitely not home to the forty acres.

Pat was the discharge planner. Pat was the name of the woman in charge of kicking my family out of St. Mary's. They were kicking us out, with our heavy hearts of badness broken in two, with our peanut butter sandwiches cut four ways and nestled in the tiny cooler with our airline-sized bottles of water. Pat was sympathetic in a way I wasn't buying. Like the bank manager who denies a loan to the family being evicted. Her words said she wanted to help, but not enough to change anything. There are no favors.

Pat said Dad had to go, by Friday, and it was Tuesday afternoon. She would send out faxes on Wednesday morning to see what nursing homes in Michigan anywhere near the forty acres would take a man in his condition. I had to ask out loud because it didn't register with me: a nursing home? But my dad was going to Nashville in September on a camping trip with my mom; he had only a few weeks before they left, it being mid-July now. So we needed to focus on his recovery—even after five weeks I couldn't fathom any other future state for him. A nursing home in Hillman, a dinky little town in Northern Michigan, would definitely not work. A nursing home in Gaylord, MI would not do either. Mom and I got in the car Wednesday morning to head for St. Mary's. Our situation was desperate. We didn't have any answers. I looked over at her in the passenger seat. In my life I had sensed utter desperation in Mom only twice. And both of those desperate moments came after my dad's stroke. Both times, I had to do whatever I could to make that feeling in her go away, because I couldn't live with it—I couldn't stand to fail her. I would do anything—anything I had to do not to fail her.

What happened on the way to St. Mary's that day was nothing short of a miracle. We knew whatever we came up with, this was our only chance; we had to have this situation figured out by the end of Wednesday, or my dad would be heading to a nursing home in northern Michigan where he would surely die. He would die because my mom had promised my dad she would never let him end up in a nursing home. We had to keep that promise, no matter what it cost us.

We found out about this place we called the "limbo" hospital from Greg. Greg was a pilot friend of Scott's, someone he met in flying school. Greg's sister, Janet, was a nurse at a hospital in Troy and had heard of an interim care facility where people can go if they are not ready for rehabilitation but are being discharged from the hospital. Greg called me Wednesday morning on our drive to St. Mary's and gave me the number for Select Specialty Hospital at St. Joe in Ypsilanti. We called them as soon as we got to St. Mary's and asked what we had to do to get in. It wasn't guaranteed. They had to evaluate, and then he could go only if they had space. There were no promises. They came to evaluate my dad Wednesday morning; by Wednesday afternoon Dad had been accepted. An ambulance would arrive Thursday morning to pick him up and drive him from Saginaw to St Joe. We had done it; we had saved him. It felt like a miracle. The woman from Select Specialty who came to meet us might as well have been an angel dropped straight from Heaven. I wanted to hug her and cry with relief. I knew Select Specialty didn't accept us because they wanted to save my mother from desperation and erase from me the heartache and overwhelming anxiety that came from our situation, but nonetheless, they gave us the answer we needed and it was as if the solution had fallen right out of the sky into our laps. It felt like a victory that was greater than any victory I had ever known. And when someone is as grateful as we were, it seemed impossible to convey. Like anytime we as human beings impact others' lives profoundly, we don't always realize how much. People are thankful; they thank profusely. They embarrass us a little bit. We thank them back. We say it was nothing. We move away a little because it's too much. They are left to realize they are still desperate, in a way, because they are so grateful. And though gratitude is a beautiful thing, the world does not by nature see gratitude as a measure of strength. It is still one step from desperation. It comes from meeting the edge of the end and clawing to hang on. It is not the emotion of the robust and vital.

Greg's sister, Janet, did not understand how grateful we were. She was undone by our gratitude. She seemed even a little put-off. But that was okay. I forgave her, because I'm guessing she later experienced her own moment of gratitude that was met with disdain. Her brother Greg died three years later of liver cancer, just like Mom. He was diagnosed with his disease three days after Mom's death and died the following year, just a week short of our first anniversary without her.

When Mom and I found out that Dad was going to Select Specialty in Ann Arbor and not going to a nursing home in Hillman, it happened to be a very sunny and warm afternoon. It was midsummer, and we felt like we had won something bigger than either of us ever knew we would fight for. We jumped up and down; we left the hospital feeling an elation that hadn't been in our hearts for weeks, or maybe ever. On the way home to the forty acres, we stopped at Lucky's Steakhouse, off an exit just north of Saginaw. We had history here, at this exit. My parents and I had met there many times when I went to college in Ann Arbor and didn't want to drive all the way home but still wanted to see my parents. It was a great compromise when we missed each other but were short of time. This exit meant different things now; I tried not to think about the history. So much of our lives now were spent not thinking about what was before, but also not talking about how we weren't thinking about it, because all of that hurt in a way we simply could not face.

We called Grace to tell her the good news. We ordered dinner— fish and chips. Neither of us noticed they brought us chicken strips instead. We ate most of the meal before either of us stopped to really pay attention to what we were doing. We were too busy in our celebration spending a few minutes breathing in and out—and calling relatives who would want to know. I think I may have called Melanie to tell her, but honestly I only remember talking to her only twice, both at St. Mary's. The first time was when the stroke happened. The second time I was outside, in the grass, watching Mom eating a peanut butter sandwich quarter while sitting on the grass in the sun, and looking tired. Melanie told me I was doing a nice job managing the situation. I didn't believe her words entirely, didn't take them at face value. Then somewhere between St. Mary's and Select Specialty, Melanie lost her desire to be gracious. She wrote an e-mail to Mom telling her it must be nice that we all were spending time together, and how she would have liked to have been included. I wondered what exactly she was waiting for. The stroke hadn't come with an invitation for any of us. We just showed up. We put aside anything that would interfere with our ability to be there, for them. Mom didn't answer Melanie's e-mail. She was too tired. Mom lost her ability to be strong in the face of Melanie. And I lost my patience.

12

We've Got Plans

Somewhere between the first few days and the third week after my dad had his stroke, and we were driving back and forth an hour and a half to the hospital every day, there came a realization that I didn't know when this would end. I didn't know what would happen next. I didn't know where this situation would lead. My mom was an only child and she cared for her parents as they aged, culminating in my grandmother's death from pancreatic cancer. My grandmother lived her last days lying in Melanie's bedroom, the back corner bedroom of the house with red carpet and dark paneling, the bedroom that looked out over the majority of the forty acres. The room where we went to turn on the attic fan in the summer to cool off the house, the room where my mom kept her orchids; the ones Melanie and Jed sent her for Mother's Day and her birthday through the mail, all packed and kept cold until they were unveiled upon arrival. Mom could grow flowers like magic and her gardens were an extension of her my entire life. She had bushes of lilacs that grew along the north edge of the mowed yard. I always believed, my whole life, those lilac bushes represented something about me, specifically. I can't remember if my mom told me she planted them around the time I was born or that they just flowered in late May near my birthday, which made her think of me. But those lilac bushes made a connection between us. Those bushes started out small and they grew and I made sure to be home on at least a few occasions as many years as possible when they were in bloom.

During our trips back and forth after my dad had his stroke, we didn't know what to think and we didn't know where this would go, so we acted like this situation was very temporary. Somehow Dad would be back; what mattered to him at the forty acres must be preserved, because when he returned he would need it to be as it was—because enough other things for him would be hard. His long recovery back, his permanent loss of left arm usage; maybe he would have a limp. Our only real experience with strokes was my grandfather, who started out a mechanic with his own repair garage in Flint when my mom was little. Back at a time when Flint was bustling with workers and people who went to the auto factories every day. When Flint had families living in little houses with pretty shutters and yards that were fenced and wives who wore skirts and aprons, my mother was an only child with a best friend named Gale. He lived next door. Tony was my mother's dog; a little springer spaniel, black and white, who was featured in one of our family collages I made when I was a teenager. Tony was a part of the framed photos, just like the photo of my mom as a baby on her father's shoulders, and my grandmother looking graceful and gorgeous in her lipstick and pretty dress, legs crossed, sitting in the easy chair staring at the camera, her chin resting on her hand.

My grandfather had a stroke when I was in my twenties, in college, so I don't remember much about it but I do remember my grandfather continued to be a similar guy to the one he was before the stroke. He just held his left arm closer to his body, like it was sprained or something. He limped a little bit. He slurred his words and the left side of his mouth was weak; it hung low. He had trouble swallowing. I wrote a poem in college about how he choked on his peas. I got an A. That poem was the beginning of the realization of loss. I had stayed away from visiting my grandmother when she was sick and living at my parents' house. When it was over and she was gone I regretted it; I still regret it. Regrets are things we can't take back. I have a couple more regrets in my life. Times I wasn't where I should have been. Places I wasn't when I needed to be. One thing I know for sure, when the end comes for my dad, I'll be there. I'll be there from now on.

These experiences with my grandparents were all Mom and I had to work with. It was all we knew as far as what might come next. And if my dad had come back to life after the stroke and been more like my grandfather, Mom might have been able to handle that. She knew what that looked like. But anything else, we didn't know. The only other thing we knew was death. We knew cancer, and what comes next. We were going to find ourselves more experienced with that again, before long. But for now, at this point, all my mom and I knew was my dad was lying in a bed in a hospital and that didn't fit into the plans. They had camping trips already paid for coming up in a few weeks. They needed to get in their motorhome and start heading south. Dad always drove. He needed to be able to drive. Dad had fallen off a pickup truck at my Uncle Mick's a few years ago and broken his heel. His foot was stiff a lot of the time, but he managed. He was stubborn about it. He didn't like being kept from doing what he wanted. He didn't like aging. He fought it. And what happens when a person fight things and doesn't appreciate how beautiful and free life is, that person ends up with a watershed stroke on the right side of his brain. It paralyzes his left side and leaves him aphasic, and he wears a diaper. He can't walk. Then his wife dies, and he leaves his house for the last time. All because he didn't appreciate what God and the Universe gave him. But he didn't know that would happen. He would have changed how he acted if he had known. He is a humble man, really. He doesn't ask for much. He never wanted much, just his freedom. He taught his daughters to want it too.

In late June, Scott and I went home one day after driving back and forth from the forty acres to the St. Mary's neuro-intensive care unit and we realized we would need to get some items from Ann Arbor and come back. One of those items would be our kitty, Maia, who was old and lonely and would enjoy the forty acres in summer, lying on my parents' back deck in the sun. Their deck didn't have a gate, and she could fit through the spaces between the wooden posts. We didn't want to just let her out there because she might run away. We adopted her when she was old, twelve or thirteen at least according to the vet. She had been a stray for years until someone finally called animal control and told them to pick her up. She was ragged and matted and skinny, but the animal control staff could see her potential. They called the local animal rescue that promptly sent a foster family over to pick her up. There she stayed, in the foster home, for two years until I happened upon her one day at the local PetSmart where the foster organization was showing off their adoptable animals. I was grieving the loss of Cerin and thought a new pet might do me good. I drove over to the Pet Smart to see a particular dog that was advertised, but he had already been adopted. There were lots of other dogs and cats and I wandered through the aisles, aimlessly, enjoying the little faces. On my way out, I wandered by a sleeping cat in a small cage. The name on the cage was Maddie, an acronym for all the things she was and had been—matted, adaptable, darling, whatever. I don't remember what the acronym was, I only know I was walking by and something made me stop. And that's how I ended up with Maia.

I thought the best way to keep her from escaping the deck would be to nail some chicken wire to the deck posts; we had done this on our Ann Arbor deck and it worked great. Maia wasn't looking to escape, but like a lot of animals, given the opportunity for more freedom she would choose to push the limits. But put up a barrier, even plastic chicken wire, and she was happy to obey. I found some small finishing nails in the garage and was in the process of securing the chicken wire on the deck when my mom walked out into the sun porch and gasped. "Your father wouldn't want you to put those nails in the deck," she said. "He was planning to finish the wood later this summer and now it will have holes in it." I stopped, a little surprised. *I don't really think Dad will be worried about it now*, I thought to say, but didn't. It was the first time I realized I was starting to see the reality of things. Mom wasn't.

13

The Boyfriends

When I was six or seven years old, Melanie brought a boy-friend home from college on Christmas break. We had squirrels nesting in our attic. We could hear them scurrying around in the ceiling. We had an attic fan with a vent up near the roof that provided them an entryway, making our attic a great place to live in the winter if you are a squirrel.

One day over the break while Melanie and her boyfriend, who after this particular visit I never saw again, were sitting in the living room watching TV. My sister was on the couch reading and the boyfriend was lounging in the orange La-Z-Boy. I was in my room playing alone. I had a pencil in my hand because I was drawing or writing or something, and I heard the scurrying in the attic. I jumped and whacked the ceiling with the pencil, hoping to scare away the squirrels. I held the pencil end in the palm of my hand since I wasn't tall enough to reach the ceiling otherwise. When I jumped, I jammed the pencil lead into the soft flesh of my palm. Immediately the lead broke off, and my hand was bleeding.

I knew it was a stupid idea to jump; it was just one of those dumb things kids do. Now I was startled and in pain and knew what I had done would get me into trouble, but I needed to tell someone. I had to tell someone who could help me clean it out and bandage it up and make sure I wasn't going to die of lead poisoning. This was one of those situations in my childhood where, given a less painful situation, I might not have told anyone just to avoid the fall-out. Especially if Melanie was home, because most of the time if Melanie was home that meant Mom and Dad were barely speaking and Grace was in her room hiding. On the numerous occasions I did something stupid while Melanie was home, like spill milk at the dinner table or jam a pencil lead in my hand, I was sure to be yelled at if anyone found out.

But I had an idea. This stranger, this relative stranger would help me. He was a nice guy, a good guy, I could tell. As the little sister of someone who basically disliked kids, especially her pain-in-the- neck youngest sister, I was very good at picking out adults who would help. I don't know what it was about him, but he must have given me the sense he would take care of things. I don't know. For whatever reason, he was my first choice for someone to go to about the lead in my hand.

His feet were extended out on the foot rest of the La-Z-Boy, and he was reading a magazine or book or the newspaper. I crawled up on the lap of this relative stranger with my bleeding hand squeezed tightly shut. With gentle concern, he asked me what was wrong. I wouldn't say anything. I wouldn't show him my hand. He took ahold of it—not roughly or with judgment, but in a way that made me trust him. I don't even know what to make of that, so many years later—this relative stranger seemed safer than anyone else in my house. He grasped my wrist and opened my hand so my palm was flat, the pencil lead buried, blood drying around the wound. He seemed worried--as much as any college-age boy would be when his girlfriend's little sister crawls up on his lap with a bleeding hand.

I can't recall at all what happened after that. My guess is they turned me over to my mother, who was busy cleaning house or planting flowers or doing laundry or otherwise avoiding a situation that would put her in regular close proximity with Melanie and her guest. But they must have been done with me by then. The bleeding little sister, as cute as I might have been for crawling in his lap, I was all bloody-palmed and crying and I'm sure they didn't want to be stuck taking care of it. I'm sure they asked me the obvious question. Mom was accustomed to my antics, like falling down the basement stairs and getting a bloody nose, or tripping over the dog and spraining my elbow. Whatever I could say that would keep me out of trouble—true or not—would have been my story of choice; that much I know for sure.

Melanie had other boyfriends she brought home over the course of my childhood. The one who helped me with my bleeding palm was the first one I remember. The other two came later. One somehow ended up on a Christmas visit to my grandparents in Florida. I haven't any idea why Melanie would have brought a boyfriend, but I must have been around ten or eleven by then and much too old to sit on a stranger's lap. We were in my grandparents' travel trailer, the one they pulled behind their sedan each year on the way down to Zephyr Hills. It couldn't have been big enough to hold us all, but somehow it must have. I can imagine the scent of the air, the smell of cornstarch powder and sizzling bacon, like all my grandmother's houses. I was too old to sit on the boyfriend's lap, but it was kind of a family joke. Everybody expected it of me. There I was, probably only at the trailer for a matter of hours since our two-day journey from Michigan to Florida in the back of the pickup, Grace and me. Sitting in his lap, they would have teased me, there would have been chastising from my parents, and I would have gotten up and sat somewhere else.

The feeling of it, the joke, them poking fun, it's a vivid feeling. But it was a turning point in my childhood too, like the first time I was made aware. I was nine and I had started to develop early. In my whole life all summer long I hadn't worn a shirt or shoes unless absolutely necessary. I knew in my heart I couldn't get away with it again that year. But I made a little show of it that spring to see what she would say. My mother's disgust was palpable. She immediately sent me in to put a shirt on. You can't go without a shirt anymore, she told me. She never thought about how it came across to a pre-teen, developing adolescent. Stuff like this happens to everybody at that age. Everything is harder at that point in life, but I think we forget how vulnerable those moments are when a person is going from youth to young adult. It's not hard to feel bad about what you are becoming and almost anything said or done can make it worse. I'm sure my mom went through it too, when she was young.

The last time I remember one of Melanie's boyfriends was much more recently. I was an adult living in Ann Arbor in my own apartment. Melanie was in Philadelphia. There was a short period of time—four or five Christmases at most--when we were all home together for the holidays. Grace was getting divorced, so she started coming home alone. I was single and in my twenties. One year, Melanie and her latest boyfriend, who owned a used car lot, came home to visit. I picked them up at the Detroit Metro Airport and they stayed at my house for one night before we drove up to West Pine.

I don't recall a thing about their stay, but one moment sticks in my head: we were driving out of Ann Arbor and they started arguing about something. I cut in, laughing, making some kind of very neutral joke to break the tension. It was during a point in my life when I felt like I was on track to win some kind of Nobel Peace prize for being so closely aligned with my life's purpose. I was volunteering as a counselor for a youth group; I went to Haiti for several weeks and helped build a school; I was working at a job for a start-up company that I really enjoyed. My happiness with life showed through in my interactions with them, because they commented on how I had diffused things, and the role of mediator I perfectly fulfilled. I wish to this day I could remember exactly what Melanie and her boyfriend said, because I think it was the time in my life I felt like I had done something that impressed her, and made her feel proud.

14

Like Life, or Not

ad was in inpatient rehab for six months. When he first made his way to Oak Glen rehabilitation facility after our second miracle happened and the tracheostomy tech at Select Specialty decided Dad could breathe without the tube in his neck, and therefore could go from Select Specialty to rehab, we moved to the next impermanent location in our journey. We thought it would feel more like home, more normal than the hospital, and we expected it would be a nice place because of all we had heard. But when we finally got there it just seemed like a tiny dorm room--or worse, a hospital room with a roommate that's too close in proximity. There was no privacy and no space to spread out or feel comfortable. It did have the effect of throwing us into the real world again, for the first time, and what we discovered was we didn't feel ready, none of us. It was mid-August and the baseball games were still going on and football was starting—Dad's two favorite sports. But the sight of a baseball game made me think of St. Mary's and brought back what it felt like to walk into the hospital room for the first time; his head cocked at an unconscious angle, staring up at the dark TV screen. Fall was right around the corner, and we had only just heard my dad's voice for the first time since June 24. They finally removed the respirator and the tracheostomy. We were warned his voice might sound different from months of plastic and metal in his throat. We were warned that respirators and tracheotomies tear up the vocal chords and what is left heals and sometimes what comes out of healed vocal cords is not the voice you remember from childhood and adulthood and all the years of life that you have known this person. We wondered what might be his first word. Before he talked, we didn't really know if he would even be himself. But his first word was "Scott," spoken as soon as he saw us walk through the door of his room at St. Joe the day they removed the tubes, the day before he left for Oak Glen.

Select Specialty had been a nice place, new and clean and modern. Oak Glen was old and outdated and the wallpaper was fading. Oak Glen was the first time we would see what rehab meant, what getting back to life as a person who had to live in the body and mind he was left with would be like. Each step we took in life post-stroke was like a journey of thousands, a monumental trek that started over each time we moved from location to location. Part of what changed was the driving route my mom would take from the rented house on Davis to the new hospital, or rehab, or wherever she had to go. I drew her handwritten maps; the corner where she started would be a little house with a colorful roof and Samantha waiting in the window. Each street and turn was a color, the arrows pointing her to the other end of the paper, her location. I wanted to believe the maps helped her, but what I knew was they helped me. The colored pens made the map seem like a drawn picture from a child, from someone who loved her dearly. I kept those colored pens for a while after she died, and then I gave them to Kara's youngest daughter, Mary.

By the time Dad got to Oak Glen, his only food since June had been through a feeding tube. He hadn't so much as sipped water into his mouth since all of this happened. Strokes often cause problems swallowing—and sometimes people never get off the feeding tube. There was a tracheostomy specialist at Select Specialty, Jessica, who knew how desperate we were to get him to rehab. But rehab won't take someone with that level of equipment; he would have to go to a nursing home if he couldn't be weaned from it. No one seemed very concerned about this, except my mom, my sister, me, and Jessica. Four days before my dad was to leave Select Specialty, the discharge coordinator came to us. Her name was Kim. She was not as bad as Pat, but nonetheless, we had decisions to make--and fast. She told us if the tracheostomy was gone, Oak Glen could take him. Jessica found this out through Kim, and cared enough to try. She refused to believe he couldn't get better. She wanted the tubes out of his body. She believed in him like we did, and she wouldn't give up. She took the tubes out of his throat and checked his blood oxygen every hour on the hour. He only had to make it from Friday to Monday, 72 hours, without dropping below a level that meant he needed the extra help. He had to have a swallow test so we would know he could eat something by mouth, which would mean we could get rid of the feeding tube. Select Specialty had made it clear he had to go by Wednesday, no other options, so this all had to work. My dad passed with flying colors, because he had to, because he was more than tough, more than stubborn, and even if he couldn't talk and we didn't know if or when he would again, he had to make it to rehab. And he knew it too. Rehab, then the forty acres, that's what we told him. That was his truth. That's what he wanted more than anything.

We moved him out of Select Specialty on Wednesday. The ambulance took him directly to Oak Glen dressed in a hospital gown, lying on a bed pad, naked from the waist down. He hadn't worn regular clothes since June 25. He hadn't sat up on his own without assistance since June 25. His legs were shriveled, his back was weak; his coordination was gone. He had gone from driving himself to the hospital in June to lying prone on his back, bed sores growing on his ankles and back and tailbone by the day. He hadn't had a haircut in three months. The father I grew up with, who showered and shaved himself every day had not been cleaned other than from his bed with a washcloth by a nurse for nearly ninety days. Every time they came in to change him, we left the room. Every time they came to check for wounds, we left the room. He would not experience for a while yet the humiliation of having his family change his brief. We would not feel the frustration of being forced to spend twenty-four hours straight at the hospital being watched by the staff as we took care of Dad ourselves, just so a doctor who didn't want him to be released to home would be forced to give my mom the okay to take him home. They would fight us all the way, and my mom would fight back. In the end, she would win. We didn't yet know that this aphasic man who would repeat each thing we said to him three times would not be able to stand the sight of his own face, and would scream and yell at the sight of himself, as if he were fighting for his very life.

Oak Glen was, for us, what it must have felt like to my grandfather when he drove his obstinate young son away from the tiny town of Woodmoor, MI where all of his family lived, and dropped him off in downtown Detroit, on the corner, and drove away: bleak, depressing; terrifying. Taking my dad to Oak Glen was like being on a street corner with no money and no friends and no winter coat on the first of November, in a strange town, in a foreign land. We searched in our heads and hearts for what we had known of him. We clung to who he was before the stroke—someone who loved football, and laughed, and told stories; who watched baseball and hated more than anything to be fussed over. This man could no longer talk; he pushed away with disdain the small TV on the electronic arm that hung above his bed. It hurt his head. It hurt his eyes. He hated it because it wasn't what he remembered and he knew there was a problem, but he couldn't speak the words.

The physical therapist showed up an hour after we arrived at Oak Glen. It was obvious in her face that she was seeing just some other old guy who had a stroke and wouldn't recover and should be in a nursing home somewhere instead of sitting here, in front of her, with his family looking at her, waiting for the miracle to happen. What she didn't know is our heavy hearts of badness had broken a long time ago and still we refused to give up. We would make it through this part too. She didn't yet know who she was dealing with, because my mom was about to start asserting herself. After months of talking to intensive care nurses and doctors who gave us only the tiniest incremental hope, we were tired of it all. We wanted to go home. More and more we had started to feel something had gone terribly wrong at St. Mary's—that something we would never know for sure may have happened there that wasn't anything we could ever confirm. We thought perhaps, from the notes in Dad's chart that when the surgeon went in to clear out the carotid arteries that were full of gunk, that something hadn't gone well and so they had stopped, closed him up, knowing a chunk of globous goo had likely escaped and would end up in his brain, choking off the blood supply somewhere. So they kept him in recovery for four hours, and yes, it happened just as they thought. So here they had a man who was older by age standards, because that's what you are if you need carotid artery surgery–you are older and you have had a life already, hopefully a long life. You have a family in the waiting room expecting you to be part of the ninety-six percent of carotid artery surgeries that come out just fine. Forty-five minutes to suck out the junk, two hours in recovery, a few days in the hospital and you go home with scars on your neck and hopefully a few more years added to your already long life.

But that isn't how it happened. Dad was part of the four percent who don't make it out in forty-five minutes but who end up either dead or something else. He was the something else. We were all part of the something else. Life as we knew it was all over now. That was something I would revisit later, without any way to fix it and I would know I couldn't, wouldn't do anything about it—I wouldn't go back to that surgeon and ask him for answers. It was all too late and he couldn't have done anything about it anyway. The globous goo was growing too long, without intervention, and really the person most responsible for that was my dad himself. Now we were at Oak Glen, and the feeding tube was gone, and the tracheostomy was gone, and the respirator was gone, and it was just him. We just had him, the new him, like a brand-new baby, and we were just beginning to know what life would be.

Our first roommate at Oak Glen was on his way to being discharged when we arrived. Like most people in rehab, it's a relatively short visit and all they left behind was a comfortable throw pillow and a stool with a crocheted cushion my mom used each day, the pillow to support her back while she read and my dad slept. The stool was perfect for resting her feet. I wish I would have taken the stool with me when we left Oak Glen. It wasn't ours, but it was left for us, and my mom used it to make herself feel comfortable. It seems somehow precious now. The second roommate we had was a personal friend of my dad's regular nurse aide, Pat. She took her job very seriously. At this point in our journey, we didn't know about changing briefs, or bed baths, or the nuances of caring for someone in my dad's condition. At this point we still thought in our heavy hearts of badness that he would eventually get better, a lot better, and would walk again. He would go home and my parents would live a lesser life, but it would be some semblance of the life they had. We did not yet know that instead it would be my mother who died first, and after she died it would fall to me to change what he excreted into multiple briefs each day, roll him and change him and clean him, feed him, read to him. Pat could have taught my mom things, but I quickly could see that wouldn't happen. Not because Pat was a mean woman or a cruel woman, but because she was a woman who had her own difficult life, her own difficult relationships with her family, her husband, her children; a woman who looked for people who needed her, and found them in her rehab patients at Oak Glen. She needed to be needed there. She would not give that up for my mother.

15

It's All Over Sometime

Pat and my mother did not get along well. My mom felt threatened, I think. This woman could give my father more of what he needed at that moment than Mom could, and it seemed like Pat flaunted her regular interactions with my dad a little, calling him by a pet name, and caring for him in ways my mom didn't feel comfortable. Pat was lucky. She went into this career willingly, and came across my dad for a patient. My mom was not so lucky. She did not ask for this situation and she most certainly did not feel equipped to handle it, even if she would never admit it. My mother was strong in many ways, but she could be vindictive and petty. Melanie was half my mom and half my dad and I always thought she got the worst halves of both. My mom wanted my post-stroke dad to be the man she met and married: the strong guy who held up his half of the bargain, who could take care of her when needed, who was a partner—not a helpless person. Mom didn't like helplessness.

She didn't value weakness and didn't suffer people who used drama as a lifestyle and wore it like a dress. That was Melanie-- always the center of attention, always dramatic and full of complaints. Mom liked happy and chipper and eager-to-please people. I learned that fast and stuck with it as a survival mechanism. It served me well in my growing-up years.

I can't remember if Mom ever actually complained about Pat to the nursing staff or anyone else. I know she didn't hide her disdain very well, but she veiled it enough to get through the days at Oak Glen. When a man Pat was caring for as a side job ended up needing rehab, he was admitted to my dad's room as his roommate. I thought Mom's head would pop off—now Pat would be around Mom and Dad that much more, and commented on having her "two men" in one place. Mom used a high-pitched fake voice to imitate Pat's comments. I never actually met this roommate, because he came in on an evening shift and I had already left to go home. Mom always showed up at Oak Glen around 8:00 in the morning and left around 3:30 in the afternoon. I didn't go see my dad every night after work, but I talked to my mom every night for an update. I think Pat's "other" guy made it through the next day, and then inexplicably died during that next night. Apparently a young nurse at Oak Glen, Rachel, who was not a nurse's assistant like Pat but was a full-fledged RN, found him dead in his bed some hours after giving him his medications. Mom called me on the phone while I was at work to tell me. There was the faintest sound of satisfaction in her tone. Pat blamed Rachel for negligence. She wouldn't admit it openly, but she was happy to share her thoughts with us, whether we asked or not. Mom enjoyed the bit of gossip and the obvious way this situation distressed Pat. We wondered if my dad realized what was happening because the rooms had such close quarters, even with the curtain separating the two of them. I liked Rachel a lot. She was very matter-of-fact. She knew how steel herself from the veiled accusation that she had done something wrong. Pat wore her feelings like an outfit, so forlorn and dramatic, having lost an old man to unexplained death in his sleep that no one else seemed interested to investigate. Rachel seemed to either see it coming or knew from past experience that she had to be ready to defend herself when it came to Pat.

Oak Glen was the place where they told us they would teach Dad how to walk again. It was the place with the amazing therapists, Amy and Shelley. Amy was in her late twenties. She had been morbidly obese and had at some point had surgery to her stomach that would purportedly help her thin down. I would have never known; to see her fully dressed she looked like any other average-sized twenty-something, except for the large swaths of swinging flesh under her arms where her triceps should be. I would stare at those swaths like they were American flags hanging just down from her armpit. I tried to imagine her a hundred pounds heavier. I couldn't. Shelley was a little older--late 30s, early 40s. She had a lot of experience and she wanted progress right away. She saw potential. She saw the ability for change. She was convinced my dad would leave Glacier on his own two feet. She worked hard. She changed his brief if he messed mid-therapy session rather than send him back up to his room for the nurses to deal with. She massaged his weak leg. She used electro-shock treatments on his left arm and leg muscles to see if she could force some movement. She stood him up at the parallel bars. He still couldn't talk well, his brain was slow, so slow, and his words were slow. Too much information at once and he became angry, lashed out. His first day of therapy, there was an assistant therapist who threw a ball to him and told him to catch it. He hit her. This was not my dad, I thought. He doesn't hit or throw out of frustration. I was shocked; I wanted to protect him. My mom's reaction was muted; she stood carefully and quietly next to him, watching. She didn't say anything.

All of a sudden I was back in the summer of 1975 when my dad was fighting with Melanie in the kitchen. They were screaming at each other, and he grabbed her by the throat. My mom marched Grace and me out to the car. It seemed like a station wagon in my head, but I don't remember us having a station wagon. I climbed in and lay down. I was scared. I got in the back and tried not to think about what I just saw. I didn't feel surprised, really; I guess by that point I had seen it before but I could feel my heavy heart swelling with all the badness I was piling onto it, all the things I was learning about anger and how it seemed like something to avoid or you ended up being choked by your dad or ridiculed by your mother and riding around aimlessly in a station wagon, up and down the dirt roads that adjoined the forty acres.

Oak Glen was where the pureed food came into the picture. It is where our speech therapist Kim tried to feed my dad in vain every day. She was sweet but timid and after three months of food that came to us in the shape of the food it had been before it was blended to a pulp, like carrots, and even hamburgers, I started to wonder how this situation would ever change. He had passed his swallow test at St. Joe. Why couldn't we try something solid? But she was scared he would choke, and what did I know? Nothing, except that aspirating food into his lungs would most likely mean death after some extended illness like pneumonia. So I wanted to charge forward like the tracheostomy tech at St. Joe, but I also wanted him to live. We watched him day in and day out push away the food she brought to him twice a day during therapy. She talked to him. He tried to speak and tell stories. But his mind wouldn't let him. We learned this fast after he started to talk. He repeated everything three times and often would say no or yes—but it was just his way of filling time while he looked for the right word. Soon we figured out the staff were asking him questions and he was giving the wrong answer before had the time to follow up with his real needs—but they had already moved on. To the rest of the world, whatever word he said was the answer—it was that simple. To him, the curtains of words that hung just out of his reach would mostly elude his memory. Words were dark and inky and he couldn't quite make them out. He grew pensive and stopped trying to talk. I didn't blame him.

It was still summer when dad went to Oak Glen and Mom would bring Samantha on the weekends and we would go out to the garden with dad in his wheelchair and sit where the raised beds of tomatoes were growing, the sunflowers, and the herbs. The bird feeders were filled and chickadees would race from box to box, finches and blue birds and robins and scarlet tanagers. I pulled a tiny cherry tomato, ripe to bursting, from a plant one day. My dad was sitting in the sun, his face lined with the pain and age the stroke had placed on him. My sister was there, and my mom, and Samantha. I bit into the cherry tomato and I held it to his nose. I asked him to smell it, to smell summertime and to taste it, just lick it with his tongue. He was like a baby bird, like an infant, opening his mouth with utter trust and following directions eagerly, tasting what had been so familiar to him his whole life and what had become so far away, so lost, so forbidden in one season of his life--one long interminable summer. We still saw it only as loss. We would see it that way for a long time and some of us, my mom especially, would never see it as anything else until it was too late for her. But I couldn't blame her. For me, I was still searching for the way to save everyone when we got to Oak Glen. That job had not been done yet and I was still determined to win. Like Amy and Shelley, I was determined that somehow my fantasy would become reality, and something that didn't work would work again, magically, with a lot of elbow grease and hope in our heavy hearts of badness. I wouldn't learn to see the darkness all the way to the light for a long time yet. There was a lot more darkness to get through.

Oak Glen was where the roundabouts started. The day after my dad got there, the map I had drawn my mom became useless. It showed her the way to go, making a left onto Glacier Way from Fuller. But that intersection was closed, semi-permanently, while they put in a roundabout--four roundabouts to be exact. They would finish this project sometime after we no longer had any reason to even think about Oak Glen, but I would drive through there years later and realize those four roundabouts that took drivers over the freeway represented a mountain of obstacles to be navigated before anyone could make it to the other side. It seemed like the project might never been finished, but it was. Eventually everything gets done, one way or the other.

16

What We Did

*J*anuary 11, 2011, Dad finally moved out of all hospital systems and into the Davis house. For the first time in seven months, Mom didn't have to get up in the morning and go somewhere all day. She could stay at home with my dad. She could plan to do other things, like grocery shop. Like all the steps we took in the process, this was monumental and seemed to bring with it some element of healing, but also elements of newness that brought new problems to deal with, new issues we hadn't anticipated, new things that might prove more unpleasant or difficult than we had imagined. This time the newness was having various caregivers in the house twenty-four hours a day. As it turned out, this might have been worse than traveling to the hospital, because now my mom never had a moment alone.

The Davis house, as we called it, was a house that held for me some fond, albeit short-lived, memories. My connection to the house and my decision to move out of it when I did were things that drastically changed the course of my life after the stroke. I met Matt and Lee Stimson, the owners, when I moved back from Flagstaff and was looking for a place to rent. They were looking for people to rent a house that had been gifted to them upon the death of Matt's parents. The economy wasn't great, so selling seemed less than likely. They weren't looking to make money on it; they just wanted someone living there who would supply enough to pay the taxes and make sure the pipes didn't freeze. They were my dream landlords; it was my dream house in a dream neighborhood. They were even willing to sell it to me on a land contract, which didn't happen, but later on seemed like an opportunity missed. I think in my entire adult life I had dreamt this situation would befall me only about a million times. I didn't believe it was true or would ever really happen. I didn't think these situations were possible or were the kinds of good fortunes that came my way. Not that I thought I wasn't lucky; I always had been, but was great at sabotaging my own best interests. Then this fantastic living situation fell into my lap. And like any self-respecting individual who regularly undermines her own happiness, I made certain I didn't stay long.

I moved in during early summer 2009, and moved out by the following April 2010, two months before Dad's stroke. Nine months of bliss at the Davis House, by myself, while I was overworked and took no vacations and visited my parents exactly two weekends all year. I had no way of knowing I had just lost my last opportunity to enjoy my parents, to live the life I had known all along. I had just missed my chance to drink in the summer light at the forty acres, to wake up early with Mom and share a twisty chocolate donut from the bakery downtown, to ride on the back of the tractor with Dad as we made the rounds on the property, stopping at the neighbor's to see the wild turkey Bob had named after his son because it liked to perch on the roof of the garage just like his son had done as a teenager, peering out over the tiny lake to watch the beaver build a dam at the far edge. By the next summer, everything would have fallen apart.

The Davis house had three finished levels: the basement where the laundry was along with a full bathroom and a bedroom that never got used. Up a half level to the landing leading out to the side yard; and then three more steps to the main floor. The main floor was broken up into a formal living room, a family room, a little library that separated the formal living room from the kitchen, a bedroom, a full bathroom and a tiled mud room that led to the backyard and out to the unattached, two-car garage. The house had been built in the 1940s by a German architect and then bought by Matt's parents who lived in it for twenty-five years. Two families had made the house theirs. The German architect and his wife had grown frail, and before they grew too old to do anything about it, they turned the top floor into a separate apartment. Their son lived there and cared for them until they were gone. Matt's parents didn't bother to remodel; they simply didn't use the kitchen on the top floor. The main floor had wainscoting and wood-trimmed windows and stained glass leading to the foyer. Little hints of Matt's parents and the previous owners were everywhere: in the fireplace mantle tile decorations and the frog mural painted on the wall in the mud room.

I met Scott six weeks after moving in to the Davis House. I was getting happier and more contented with life. I had my kitty, Maia. I had a job that took up too much time. I fretted about this. I worked too many hours all summer. I came home and walked to the baseball fields two blocks from my house to sit on the bench in the sun and watch the recreational leagues play. I wondered about getting a dog.

I thought about driving to West Pine, but Fridays the traffic was bad and I had to be back to work so early on Mondays, it was never a good time to drive up for just twenty four hours.

Scott and I started dating in August and we starting traveling in October and we started making plans for our future in January and by April I was moving out of the Davis house. Maia loved Scott's townhouse, so big and airy with lots of spots to lie in the sun and have the heat from the floor vents blow in her face. I slowly moved what I needed over, and got rid of the rest of it—so many donations to the Salvation Army. My stuff was not nice or new, it was mostly used and came from Craigslist or the PTO thrift store or my garage sale trips with my friend Becky. Scott's house had clean corners and fresh carpet and paint that was white everywhere. He had leather couches with side tables that matched and a bedroom set like a grown up. He didn't sleep on a futon on the floor with a Target® brand mattress pad on top. His house was uniform pale and brown and leather and wood. My things were ceramic and colors and flowers and fabric. It would be a few years before the color and the fabric made a true appearance, but like so many things in our lives, it would unfold slowly.

I decided to be out of the Davis house prior to our trip to California to run the Big Sur Marathon. We had planned a several day excursion that would involve flying into San Francisco, driving down the coast to Carmel, running the race, and then traveling back up to Napa and Sonoma before heading home. I wanted to be settled so when we got back it was to one household, not two. This is where fate took a turn that may have changed the course of everything. Had I been less organized and determined to make our home one space, I would not have moved out in April. That would have led to me to packing up and starting my move closer to summer, but not likely before my birthday in late May. That might have led to me waiting to move until we returned home from the trip with my parents in June; the camping trip that was cut off by the call from Mom on Friday morning, June 24, 2010. If I had procrastinated my packing and move due to work and our new relationship and training for the marathon, I might have still lived in the Davis house June 24, and Dad would have had his stroke, and then I would not have thought about moving at all. I would have stayed there, living upstairs while Mom lived downstairs. I might have even stayed after that, keeping Dad at the Davis house after Mom died, or maybe not. But my world would have moved in a different direction, of that I am sure.

There are times I miss the house on Davis, mostly because of what it represented to me. I miss my biggest problem being I am working too many hours with no vacation in sight. The never-ending difficulties of a single woman with financial woes might, even for a time, have been something I would have traded for the reality of Dad's stroke, and soon after Mom's cancer. But now that it's happened and we have made it through and our lives have taken on a reality that has become our new normal, I don't know that I would change anything. I roll over in my mind what I would give up to have stayed at the Davis house and had life remain as it was before Scott, and I can't come up with something I want to leave behind. I like to trust that is a good thing, for once in my life I want to give up nothing, I have both feet in. The inevitable things that have happened—the end of lives and the loss that equates to change are all things that would happen no matter what. I have learned they are not the parts of life to fear, after all, because then fear is all you feel if you think too much about anything. Fear becomes your driver, your catalyst. I want to believe that if I get sick or when I have lived my life and my journey here is over I will have learned to accept what is coming, because it might just be as bad as you think it will be, but you get through. You go through. There is a moment in so many things in life—your first kiss, the first time you have sex, your first public speech, your first dive into a pool, your death—when you reach the point of no return, when you cross the threshold and then you have done it, it's done. That's the only second you can let yourself feel fear, but if you are ready, if you have practiced and thought about it and prepared, in all those cases, that moment is both fear and living and experience all colliding, and then the moment is done.

17

Secrets

The Davis house presented new challenges, like all the interim steps from Neuro-Intensive-Care-to-Forty Acres would. Since I had moved out in April, Matt and Lee had found a young, single nurse with a cat named Tom to move in to the upstairs portion of the house. They were holding the bottom floor for Lee's dad to move in at some point in the near future. He lived in Texas on his own, was diabetic and sickly, and had no family nearby. There was a brother, apparently, in Austin, but Lee's father lived elsewhere, and Texas being Texas, they might as well have lived across the country due to the sheer distance between them. But in the meantime they were willing and happy to have my mom move into the downstairs, mere weeks after I had left the place. Going back to Davis to prepare it for my mom to move in was a whirlwind, like everything we were going through. But this was different, even yet. Davis had been my sanctuary and the first time I felt at peace, even though it was short-lived by my own doing. I had decorated it with all of my belongings and had brought into it people and things I would never see again. People, especially. Like The Chef—a guy I met and dated before I knew Scott (formerly known as The Pilot before I made my decision to date him over The Chef). I had left the house on a whim, believing Scott to be the right thing for me, but also knowing I had made this mistake before, over and over again, leaving my house for someone else's and giving away my things only to find myself packing up my car and reinventing a new space with new things all over again. This time with Scott felt different and I didn't know why at the time, but of course there were plans for me--for us--that would surpass any trivial wishes of living alone or having my own space again.

Going back into the Davis house, no longer with the things I had only weeks ago, and having to make a space for Mom made me have to face for the first time a place I had left without being 100% sure. There had been other places like this in my life, like the house in Flagstaff that looked out over the canyon. The basement I rented and loved, fully furnished except for my bed and Cerin's. I had been stung by a bee there while tucking Cerin into his bed one night. The bee, drugged from the cold nights and lateness in the season had wandered under the dog blanket on the floor and was clinging dazedly when I bent down on my knee, startling it. I remember the pain of the sting and the shock of it. I don't know why that sticks with me; a foreshadowing maybe. But I had loved that little place and I had left it for good reasons, similarly to why I left Davis. I didn't run, exactly, from Flagstaff. I left what I knew was there to come back to a place I knew I would be happier. In the end it was for all the reasons I couldn't yet see, but that would be true sooner than later: my parents needed me. When I left the Davis house it was for my future, for a place I couldn't get as long as I stayed in Flagstaff, no matter how much it was the answer to all my wishes as a single girl. Why those youthful wishes seem to always be granted at the wrong time--the worst time--I'll never know.

My mom moving into the Davis house was the continuation of the ways I would stretch to give them what I thought I had always failed to give—a sense of myself as capable, responsible, invincible, and a rock they could hang on to in any storm. I made Matt and Lee promise they wouldn't tell Mom that I was paying them rent to let her stay there. I asked them to lie, and they did. They told my mom it was just empty and they would keep it for their own daughters to move into some day but in the meantime it was just their charitable gift to us, something they knew we needed and they had to share. My mom didn't buy the story entirely, but she was willing to let it go with a smile and a thank you because she had bigger worries. She wasn't used to having to spend what little money they had on things they didn't really need. They had always spent their money wisely and lived a nice but frugal life. They had a house up north, a perfectly good house sitting empty that they had lived in for the last 40 years. She was worried about the costs of all of this, and was working to keep their household intact up there while having to focus on my dad's continuous care down in Ann Arbor. She couldn't think about the details of why the Davis house might be inexplicably free.

In preparation for her moving in, I rummaged for furniture where I could find it. I still had a futon bed that I had kept in the spare bedroom at Davis on the main floor. Mom and Dad had slept in it when they visited to watch my seasonal choir concerts. I put the house back together for her, and hung some pictures that I had stored in Scott's basement while I figured out what I was keeping and what I was not. This part of the journey felt like it moved fast, maybe because there were so many things I could do—not just drive back and forth from a hospital, but actually do something—make something, a household, a space for Mom to feel comfortable. She had always talked about living in Ann Arbor, having been a city girl before she met my dad. She found the country life peaceful, but I think she also enjoyed shopping with her mother as a young girl, and all the things city life brings: free classes at the library, music in the park and organic food stores with aisles for wandering. The Davis house suited her perfectly with its many windows and corner yard. I thought she would love it and I felt like I was giving her something, I wanted her to feel like I was giving her something that she had always wanted and could finally have. I was intentional in my deco-rations; I set up the cable service, though I hadn't had cable when I lived there. I was helping my mother, the woman I had known and loved for all my life.

What I forgot, and what I would glimpse on a few occasions in the last years and months and then days of her life, was her other side. We all have that other side. She kept it from me most of the time and I chose to ignore it the rest of the time. I liked to believe 100% in the secret club she and I had, the special club that shut out everyone save my father—he came first in her life when the push-ing came to the shoving. I saw that when I brought the nails out to be pounded into the wood of the deck on the back porch. But I was wrong ever to want a club that shut out my sisters, or that made me special. I was wrong, but it took me a long time to see that because I was the one on the inside. Grace and Melanie were not. At least that's what I liked to believe before the stroke, for all those years after my sisters moved out, when it was just me and Mom and Dad. When I came home from college or to visit after college was done, Mom and I would go to the grocery store on Saturday afternoon and up to the West Pine outdoor mall to wander, me to the Gap, both of us to Eddie Bauer, stopping off always at the mall café for No Bake cookies and coffee.

But I learned that events in life can change people; or maybe change is the wrong word. Circumstances can make people guarded, people who are not normally afraid to open up or be sweet. Their real nature might be there, buried, or maybe their real nature is what we see when the circumstances bring out something other than the veil we wear most of the time. There are many writers and poets and quotes that can be found that tell us our true selves will appear when the moments are hardest. What is hardest about these moments is they bring out more than just the true, they bring out the cobwebs and the half-truths and the person you are when no one is looking, because you are so overwhelmed you can't focus on keeping the veil. So people get all of you, and it's what they choose to remember that will label you, to them, change who they thought you were. Suddenly you'll be someone they admire or someone they didn't know or chose not to see when the veil was there.

I saw this in my mother, my mom, someone I knew behind the veil because I had seen it a few times when I was little. When her heavy heart of badness was thick and overwhelming her, the veil came off. What was interesting was to see how it all shook out in the end, the last couple of years. She was her best self when my dad was sick, the mother I knew and loved all my life. But when it was her end, when it was she who had to give it all up and it was she who was being pushed off the planet by circumstances she could not change, her badness took over like a full-metal jacket. I chose not to believe that who I saw then was her true self. I chose to keep her as the mom I knew when we were entrenched in our secret club, wandering the mall walkway, drinking coffee and gossiping about the same locals who were there every time we went in.

I'm still not sure our secret club selves weren't exactly who Mom and I really were, and are. Grace has certainly claimed more than once during our most heated arguments since becoming the parents to our parents that I am just like Mom. She may be right. I think the best of me emerged when my dad first got sick, and I think it's a better me than who I was before. But better might also mean more true to myself, and sometimes being truthful leaves me feeling worse than just wearing the veil and letting people think what they want. The veil I have worn can make me forget how to be truthful. I think that's okay sometimes.

18

Strangers among Us

anuary 11, 2011 meant one step closer to the forty acres. My dad was officially an outpatient, discharged to the Davis house and going to rehab three days a week. After almost eight months, he had made it halfway home. No more hospitals, no more tubes, no more doctors trying to prove we couldn't care for him and he needed a nursing home. My mom was proud she had passed that test, staying an entire 24-hour period and caring for him alone under the watchful eye of the nursing staff to show she could be there to change his brief, roll him and place pillows under his bottom to keep bed sores away, she could change his clothes, get him up in the hoyer lift, get him in his chair, get him back to bed. So just like having a newborn baby, now that he was at the Davis house things changed again and the responsibility for the care of Dad's body and mind and everything in between fell to Mom. And though she was strong and wanted him to come home, and had us to help her, she was still the one in charge. She was his wife, our mother, and the person we looked to for answers and next steps. This was harder than it seemed like it would be, and harder on my mom than I think we thought it would be. I had always seen my mom as strong and able to stand up to my dad because I had seen her do it many times. I had seen her set boundaries and fight when she didn't agree or didn't think it was right, whatever it was. She was a regular contributor to the local West Pine newspaper, and even the regional papers like USA Today, when she saw a cause worth fighting for. She was my mother, after all, and therefore a master of knowing things I didn't know, and having the answers when I didn't.

That role she played and played well had never been challenged in my lifetime. I had watched my dad's role change from family protector all the way down to the weakest link. Now he was the one we protected with the fierceness of lions. With every step in the journey back to the forty acres she handled the ups and downs with her usual grace, organizing transportation to pick them up each day for rehab, developing relationships with the drivers they saw weekly, making sure she had cash to tip them. She picked up Dad's prescriptions with plenty of time to before the refills ran out, kept the refrigerator full of food, and never ran out of his favorite snacks.

We had to have 24-hour home health care for at least the first few weeks my dad was at home in the Davis house-- a requirement of his being discharged. So Mom would have some assistance at least for a while, though it felt more like a disruption to her. Imagine having strangers in your living room day and night; moreover, strangers you wouldn't invite in your home if given the choice. Even a full-blown extrovert would grow tired of the additional body in the house, and Mom was no extrovert. We hired a company that was recommended by the St Joe's rehab facility. We met with them a few days before

Dad came home. Our family had always discouraged drama as a form of lifestyle, which is part of why my parents clashed so frequently with Melanie, whose world seemed incomplete without a regular dose of drama. Our first foray into the world of home health care organizations and the people they employ would soon move us into the era of non-stop drama. It's the thing Mom liked least about having my dad come home, and it didn't change after they moved back to West Pine.

Mom was an introvert by nature. She enjoyed quiet and alone time, and she most especially didn't enjoy having people she barely knew in her space. Having caregivers who spent the day and night meant she never had time to herself. When Dad was in the hospital, she could leave at the end of the day and go home, we could go out to dinner, she could read her mail, watch TV, and go to bed without interruption. As usual in this journey we were on, something we hadn't considered came along with every improvement—Dad was home with her now at the Davis house, Mom no longer had to drive to the hospital and everyone was together in a more normal setting. But there was just one caveat—now the strangers were coming to us instead of us going to them. And as any good stranger will do when thrust into the situation of getting to know someone, the caregivers tried to make conversation with Mom. She hated it. This is where her badness came out. She would gossip about the caregivers and complain to me about their eating habits, their choice of television shows, and their constant chatter. In my own bad way, I thought Mom was telling me these things because I was a member of her secret club, the club that meant I was her confidant, and because of that I was immune to her meanness.

But I was wrong. One day I was at the Davis house helping to clean up, put things away and take care of Dad. Aunt Gladys called.

Mom wandered around the house chatting with my dad's oldest living sister, filling her in on the latest news about Dad's progress. To my shock and surprise, she started talking about where they were living. Her words made her situation sound like hell. She was living in a dirty house in a bad neighborhood with barely a bathroom to use of her own. She was constantly accosted by the horrible strange caregivers and was forced to sleep in the front room of the house so everyone who came in wandered through her bedroom. None of this was true. No one ever used the front door of the Davis house for the very reason that it took them through my mom's living area, an area that was as far removed as it could be from the family room where the caregivers would watch TV but could still keep an eye on my dad, whose bed was in a room adjacent to the family room. I was stunned in a way I couldn't put into words because I had tried so hard, with my heavy heart full of badness, to make Mom's situation good. I thought we had an understanding. I thought we were in the special club together, the one that meant she had my back and I had hers, like girlfriends at prep school or cell mates in prison.

There were only three times in my life I can remember when my mom, through her actions or words, felt so far away from me that I thought I would never find my way back to her. The first time was when she caught me poking fun at her expense with my sister Grace when I was a little kid. I was no more than five at the time. She didn't speak to me for two days. She wouldn't accept my weeping apologies. She rejected my presence; she wouldn't talk. The second time I felt it was the call with Aunt Gladys. That time she took the sincerest work I had ever done in my life and made it seem like a cheap effort, and nowhere close to good enough. The third time would happen very close to the end of her life. And though I knew in my heart she was not herself by then, I saw something in her eyes, in her face, that left me feeling the same sense of distance from the woman I knew. Only this time, I would run out of chances to get her back.

My dad worked through his rehab for nearly six months. As spring arrived and the snowiest winter in Ann Arbor history finally came to an end, we were looking at my parents going home—this time for real. This time it would be the forty acres. The first week of May, Samantha was diagnosed with brain cancer after having surgery to remove a lump under her arm. Mom stoically added this to the many things she had to deal with, and took Samantha to the vet for several visits. She loved the young female vet that took care of Sam, and the vet loved my mom too. They understood each other. The veil my mom wore during her life in Ann Arbor served her well; she chose wisely and she gave her best side to most of the people she met. The day Samantha started to show signs of real dementia, wandering in circles and panting and seeming nearly blind in her confusion, I told Mom I would take her to the vet for the last time. It was an ending my mom didn't need right then.

I went to the Davis house while Mom and Dad were gone to a doctor appointment and pulled together all of Samantha's belongings. Her baby bear we bought her when we first adopted her in 1996, her dog beds, and her orange blanket we used on the furniture during trips in the motorhome and on the blue couches in the living room of the forty acres. Her dog bones, her dishes, her squeaky fuzzy bone my dad would throw for all those years at the forty acres, he in his La-Z-Boy in front of the living room picture window, her standing in the dining room with a playful growl. I piled it all in my car because this was it; she wasn't coming back home. Having all her stuff there when Mom and Dad got back from the doctor would only make it worse. I wanted to take it all on for them, whatever pain

I could. I set her in the backseat of my car for the last time, carried her into the vet, sat with her while we waited for the exam, cried with the vet as we decided what was best, and held ear in my hand, rubbing the warm fur and skin between my finger and thumb as she faded away after getting the lethal injection. When it was over, the vet tech said they would call us when the ashes had arrived. I left the office and went to the laundromat to wash the blankets, the beds, the things we could donate to the animal shelter. My sister texted and my mom called. I told them the news. I needed a drink. I went to the Davis house and we had cheese and crackers and wine, Mom and me. I sometimes try to remember the last time I did some of the favorite things Mom and Dad and I did together; I try to remember the last time I went to see them at the forty acres before any of this happened. I can't remember. I can't remember the last thing she ever texted to me, the last time she sent the double smiley-faces, her unique signature message that told me she was happy. I can remember the last time we went out to eat together, but that's because it was the Friday before she died and I think I knew well enough this was it. If only humans could somehow instinctively know to be present in moments that will be the last times we will do the things we most love.

19

Home Again, Home Again

ad was discharged from outpatient therapy in early May 2011. They could finally go home to the forty acres. We packed up the Davis house, rented a moving van with a ramp so we could get the hoyer and hospital bed in and out. We hardly had much more in the truck except for a few boxes. Moving day was warm and sunny, and also happened to be my fortieth birthday. We caravanned to West Pine, Scott driving the moving van, my parents riding with me in their old Ford Taurus. Grace drove herself up in her car. Scott and I would drive the moving van back to Ann Arbor the next day and my sister would remain in West Pine for a few days to help Mom settle in. Getting my dad in the car was something we had to be taught by the therapist. My dad had to learn, and so did we. We took a video of our successful attempts from the parking lot at St. Joe. We felt like it was another step to normalcy. We were starting to lose any hope Dad might walk again, but we didn't say it out loud--not very often, anyway.

We were moving them home; no more 24-hour caregivers, no more strangers in the house. Mom could sleep in a bed in the same room with Dad, and they could have their days just like always. I thought moving day would be the best day of our lives. But I think by then we were all just a little scared. I think somewhere in our minds it seemed like this would somehow bring back life as we had known it. Mom and Dad had been out of their own house for nearly a year— Dad had not seen the forty acres for 335 days, to be exact. This was going home; this is what we told him would happen if he worked hard and finished rehab. This was the final step. It wouldn't be easy for Mom. It wouldn't be anywhere near the same. Their friends all wanted to help—Dad's family, everyone they knew--they were all ready to welcome them back. A local West Pine carpenter and home remodeler had offered to make some changes to their house to make it wheelchair accessible. It took longer than he thought it would, but he finally finished it and didn't charge my parents anything. It was his community service contribution, he said, to a couple in the community who always helped everyone else. Friends of my parents had fronted the money for the materials. We were very grateful. We had so much to do and no time to think, just time to react because we had what felt like a newborn in a giant body that required constant care. But whenever the opportunity to show gratitude presented itself, we grabbed on with both hands.

Grace and I worried about Mom. When they first moved home, Mom accepted very little help, finding a home health care branch of the same company we used in Ann Arbor and hiring a caregiver to come in just a few hours a couple of days a week so she could grocery shop. My parents' newly remodeled bathroom had a wheel-chair-accessible shower; for the first time since my dad left St. Joe in January, he was able to have a shower. Mom cooked meals in her own oven and watch the news with my dad, who took up a majority of the space in their bedroom. She moved a full-sized mattress into one corner opposite his hospital bed so they could still sleep together in the same room, something they had done for fifty-two years. Mom seemed to enjoy the company of the new caregiver, Jeannie, much better than any of those from Ann Arbor. Maybe it was because she was there less frequently, or because Mom was back in her own community. Jeannie was chatty and warm, and Mom could get the latest town gossip from her. My dad enjoyed Jeannie too. I liked her because she was proactive about my dad's care; she was ready to keep trying to make his life as normal as possible.

Our original dream that he would walk again and be independent enough had, by now, completely gone by the wayside. I think that was a loss neither Mom nor Dad ever completely recovered from. We could have dealt with his aphasia and "who he would be," like Jill at St. Mary's had warned us about on Day One after the stroke. But we, most especially Mom, did not deal well with his paralysis. The fact that he was stuck in a wheelchair, and bedridden, and unable to move himself around, made it harder for everyone, but most especially her. He was helpless. Mom had to work a lot harder to care for him, and most importantly, this was a complete departure from the life she was used to with him. At the forty acres he was free to roam, and that's what he and my mom did, side-by-side, but doing their own thing. It's how they knew each other. Before the stroke, Dad would have said he never wanted to live life as an invalid. We knew this, but had chosen to ignore this as long as they were living in Ann Arbor, outside their normal life together.

But when we went back to the forty acres, Mom had to face the reality of what things were like now, and so did he. It was too much for both of them. They argued out of frustration and regret for what was now, and what had been before, and what they could not control. She complained to him when he had a bowel movement. He grew petulant when she didn't respond to his calling out to her immediately. She made him wait for things when he called, even though he couldn't do anything about it. He yelled at her incoherently, but with the same tone from the old days. But she cared for him fiercely like a mother tiger. She created a routine that met the new normal. But quickly it became clear the new normal they were living was difficult at best. Mom seemed more and more worn out as the summer went by. She missed the company of a dog and thought a new one would make her feel less lonely. She saw a dog advertised on the local news channel and wanted it. She couldn't remember the kind of dog, but thought the name was Pearl. I searched every local radio station, even some outside of the area, but could never find any trace of a dog like she described.

So I searched online and found a Cavalier King Charles puppy that needed a home. I had seen another dog like this and thought it was sweet, and cute, and perfect for my parents. My mom agreed that from the pictures it seemed like a great dog. I picked him up in early July 2011 and headed north to West Pine. When I arrived, my favorite aunt and uncle were visiting with their grown son and his wife. The puppy chased the flowers growing in the yard and was as cute as he could be. My uncle was smitten. My mom barely looked at the dog. I think in her heart she wanted her memories; she wanted Samantha roaming the yard and my dad sitting in his chair in the sun room drinking wine. She didn't want to be always thanking people for coming to visit, and asking for help with everything, and filling the sun room with garbage bags full of dirty briefs and wipes and rubber gloves. She was his representative now, the head of the household. She hated it. She wanted her partner back, her old dog, and her old life. We wanted that too.

Mom let Dad name the new puppy. He named it Daniel; we didn't know why; maybe because it rhymed with spaniel. Daniel would end up being a lot of work--more work that she had planned, and more work than I had anticipated. I bought a doggy door for Daniel so he could go in and out without bothering Mom. But that meant he tracked in dirt. He ran down the road to the neighbors because Dad wasn't able to train him and Mom had no time. So I spent an entire rainy, cold weekend in October burying an electric dog fence around the front yard by hand using a shovel. It didn't work. My mom appreciated all I did. But it didn't change anything. The new normal was challenging, exhausting and not a long-term solution. Grace and I went up to West Pine on alternating weekends and left one weekend of the month for my parents to be alone. We talked often about what might happen next, but this time it was un-clear to all of us. We had known from the beginning of Life After Stroke that the goal was to have Mom and Dad back to the forty acres, but now that they were there, what happened? What would we do if this didn't work out? How would we know it was time to change unless Mom told us? She was in charge. The life they lived now was completely up to her. Within months we wouldn't need to worry about knowing when it was time for the next change. It would be done for us.

My parents moved home in May; we got Daniel in July. We spent Christmas at the forty acres with the whole family together, except for Melanie and Jed, but that didn't really seem any differ-ent from any other year. The day after Christmas I went shopping at the Gap outlet store at the mall in West Pine. The sales were big; I bought a flannel pajama set for $2.99. My mom thought they were very cute—blue with mittens. I didn't know that would be the last thing I would buy at the Gap store in West Pine. It was the last trip I would make to West Pine to visit my parents in anything that could be considered a normal way.

In January 2012, Scott and I started a new exercise plan for the year. We wanted to do something just for us since our entire relationship save the first ten months were focused solely on reacting to my parents' situation. Health and longevity together were important to us, and we loved to exercise together. We decided we were going to run a half marathon every month for the entire year, along with participating in a few bike races during the summer and fall. It would be the year we focused on something else, something more for ourselves. We trained and ran our first half marathon during January in Mt. Pleasant. It was great to spend a night away from the house, away from work, away from everything. It felt good to think about something else for one night a month when we drove away from Ann Arbor and went out to eat and slept in a strange bed for reasons that had nothing to do with the stroke, but instead was entirely for our future, and our health.

The first week of February, my friend Amie won tickets to a Pistons game. The game was on a Friday night. I drove over to her house after work and as I was getting out of the car, my phone rang. It was Mom. She asked if I was busy—of course not, I told her. I knew she had been feeling sick for a few days because we had been texting back and forth. Earlier in the week, she had felt dizzy and sick at the grocery store and called a friend to pick her up. She left the car at the store and went to pick it up later. She had gone to her doctor to get checked out, and the doctor ordered a scope of Mom's digestive system. Mom called to see if I could possibly come home and drive her to the doctor the next morning. She had to check in to the hospital at 6:00 a.m. "Yes, of course I can," I told her. I walked into Amie's house. For what was the fifth or sixth time since the stroke, I had to back out of a date with Amie. I felt terrible every time it happened, but she understood that her moment would come, as did all of my friends who were stood up by me after the stroke. Amie gave me the look that said she got it, but she had often expressed her concern that I needed to think about myself once in a while too. I felt bad because for one thing, I knew this game was important to her and I was cancelling too late for her to make other arrangements; and two, she was right.

20

You'll Only Feel a Little Poke

drove straight to West Pine from Amie's house. Mom had already arranged for her friend, Bernie, to come to the house to watch over dad while we were gone. Bernie arrived at 5:30 a.m. and Mom and I left for the hospital. In an earlier lifetime, I would have been terrified by the prospect of my mother needing me to this extent. In an earlier lifetime, my dad would have gotten up with her and we probably would never have known she had the surgery unless there was a reason to tell us. But everything was different now. My parents no longer had each other to rely on. My dad was helpless without my mother, and my mother was left to take care of everything, including herself. She seemed very tiny to be holding the whole weight of this life. Before my dad got sick, nothing long-term ever went wrong with our family. Other than the struggle with Melanie, there were few things in our world that any of us chose to focus on for long. We opted to hold on to our given family roles tightly, because we knew them, they made sense; they were familiar. I had learned to be stronger on my own because of the things I hid from my family and friends. I had learned to get through heartbreaks and the loneliest of experiences, thanks to people like Melanie and Shane. But physical pain and illnesses of the body were not something our family faced often. Other than my grandparents, whom I chose avoid as they reached the ends of their lives, as regrettable as those decisions were, we didn't have long-standing or withering illnesses that would pull the family down to a place from which it could never return.

I helped Mom check in for her surgery and after she was wheeled away, I sat in the waiting room. It was still early in the morning and very cold; February 2. It was dark and still, both in the hospital and out. Mom had worked at our local hospital my whole life. I had spent many days after school listening to the radio in the car waiting for her to finish her day. I had done my homework from her office, eating snacks from the vending machine. She was a medical transcriptionist for many years, typing up X-ray and chart notes from doctor dictation. She was good at her job. I knew that, even when I was young. The original hospital in the old building in downtown West Pine had been changed into just offices and clinics. A new hospital building broke ground and was finished a few years after I moved away to college. My parents had talked about the new facility and the services offered, along with the assisted living facility built across the street. Before Dad's stroke, sometimes my mom talked about selling the forty acres, moving into town, and what that might entail someday. We never talked seriously about it, though. But here they were, in that very place in their lives, before we even could stop to make the plans needed to do any of what we had talked about all those times in passing.

After an hour or so the nurse came and got me. Mom was in re-covery. She was woozy and I was worried she would feel nauseous because she had a history of terrible experiences with anesthesia. So much so, it had stopped her from going through some important routine tests, like a colonoscopy. Twenty years ago she had one and practically choked to death on her own vomit after the procedure. She swore she would never have another colonoscopy again. She had since been put under maybe once or twice with better results. It felt good to be the one she called for help, I guess because I was the youngest kid, and not the one my family ever saw as overly respon-sible. But she called me, and here I was. I wanted her to be okay, to feel fine, to sit up and be good and have the doctor report the diz-ziness at the grocery store was just stress. We could figure that out. We could hire more help. We could think about next steps for dad. Maybe he needed to go to Rose City to the nursing home, where my mom knew the director and several of the head nurses. Stress was something we could manage. I told myself that stress was the reason she stopped drinking wine and eating cheese and crackers with me before Christmas, even though we loved to do that. Stress was why she had lost ten pounds from her tiny frame in what seemed like a matter of days since I had seen her last. We waited for the doctor.

Not long after she was done and the surgeon had completed his notes and sent the dictation to medical records, he appeared at Mom's door. She was still groggy, so he took me to the waiting room a few feet away. He told me she had acid reflux. Her throat looked fine and her stomach was okay. He was sending the results to be evaluated and would write her a prescription that would help with the symptoms. There was one last thing: she needed a colonoscopy. He couldn't see much from the scope, but felt it was important she do this right away. He didn't say why. I didn't ask for details. "Let's check her out every which way," he had said. "Okay," I said. That seemed right. Okay, we will do that.

I phoned Bernie to let her know we were done and Mom was recuperating. We would be home as soon as she could sit up and felt well enough to walk. I wanted her to take her time. I was happy. I reported the acid reflux. I called another good friend of my mom's, Alice, to tell her the news. Alice and Mom had been best friends for years. Alice was married to Max, whom I had never met. He was a crotchety old man, from what I understood. Alice's daughter Janine, who went to school with Melanie, had worked at the Gould's Drug Store when I was little. I remembered her long blonde hair. Janine died when I was in my 30s. My mom went to her funeral and to a garage sale Alice had later that summer. Mom bought me a coffee cup that had belonged to Janine. I still use it for work. I have taken it to every job from Michigan to Arizona and back. It's a Hallmark coffee cup with pink and blue writing. Janine got it when she worked at Gould's back in the 1980s. Alice wrote a letter to my mom every week they lived in Ann Arbor after my dad had his stroke. She now writes to my dad every week. I've kept several of her letters, because I know someday, someday I will want to read them again.

I sat by Mom's hospital bed as she slowly woke up, lying still and smiling. She looked tentative, like she was waiting to feel sick, but never did. I gave her a blanket to keep her warm. She talked to me; her mouth was dry. I gave her a little water. She closed her eyes. We worked our way out of the anesthetic drowse after about two hours. She finally felt comfortable enough to dress and go out to the car. I think the cold air and sunshine that greeted us helped to wake her up. We went home on empty stomachs; there was soup from a neighbor waiting for us. Homemade soup sounded good to her, she said. There were errands and things that needed to be done, but we would worry about those later. I would take care of everything; I would make everything okay. I wanted everything to be okay.

A week later, Scott and I were parking at Leslie Science Center. It was a nine-mile run day in preparation for our next half marathon in Mt. Pleasant; the second of a series of half marathons run on the dirt roads along farmland in central Michigan. These were the closest races we could find that time of year. Only the hardiest of running souls found a reason to pay to run 13.1 miles in the middle of a Michigan winter. We did it because it reminded us we were alive. As I was getting out of the car, my phone rang. It was Grace. She and Alex had gone up to West Pine for the weekend. They had filled up Dad's pickup truck with bags of trash Mom piled in the back sunroom: bags full of filthy briefs and wipes and gloves. Everyone's favorite room in the house, it's where we had watched birds and deer and caught up on stories when I would come home for the weekends. It's the room where Dad and I installed new windows one spring, where we ate dinner every night in the summer. The room I so desperately wanted to have carpeted before my high school graduation party, I had measured with loving care the square feet, including the stairs, so I could tell my dad what the cost would be. My dad had requested I do the measuring myself. He was a high school math teacher for thirty years. At the time he asked me to do the measuring work, I didn't realize it was his way of getting me to practice my math skills, all in the name of carpet. I also didn't realize it at the time, but they were planning to carpet it for my party anyway.

I stood next to the car out of the wind and listened. Grace's voice shook a bit as she told me the news. Mom had gotten a call from her doctor that morning. They had the official results from the scope they did the week before. The scope I was certain resulted in good news: she had acid reflux, and stress, and she would be fine. This is what I reported to Bernie and Alice. It's what I believed. But I was wrong. The results showed metastatic liver disease--cancer of the liver. It was metastatic because it had spread from somewhere else; likely her colon. All those years of not having a colonoscopy because of a reaction to anesthesia caught up to her. Colon cancer is a curable disease, right up to Stage 4. But once it metastasizes, there is no turning back. And so it began, again.

21

Problems, Part Deux

Scott and I drove up to my parents' house that night. Mom had an appointment on Monday morning with her doctor, and we would all be there to hear the news. It was the first of several occasions when we would all be there to hear what would come next. Those moments would dwindle as the situation progressed, but at first, we were a force. Before much time had passed at all, it became clear we weren't all needed, because the meetings were less about supporting how we would help her live than they were about seeing through the end of her journey to her death. The caregiver Jeannie who had been part of the household for a few months stayed with my dad and Daniel the dog while the rest of us went into town. It was a gray day, February 11. We sat crammed in a small room waiting for Dr. Francis, who took up most of the small examination room with her rotund stature. She gave us the news about the test results. There were many cancerous spots all over Mom's liver.

We were used to doctors giving us news that didn't tell us much; we had been sitting together listening to the results of tests, expectations stilted, since June 24, 2010. We were still raw from it all, though. We were still too vulnerable as individuals and as a family unit to believe we had to do this again. We felt like abused children or spouses; we were starting to believe all of this is just part of our existence, that we deserve the pain; that it will never leave us and we can't escape. Like victims of repeated trauma, we were still trying to heal from the last assault.

I think about how my dad might have handled this situation had he been his old self when Mom was diagnosed. And certainly I think had his life not taken the turn that it did, he would have been the one hearing this news, maybe without us kids by his side. With metastatic liver disease, it was obvious Mom had been moving down this road for a very long time before any of us knew it, including her. Most things in life happen for a reason. There would have been no way the dad we all knew before would have wanted to watch his wife of fifty-two years die of cancer. Lucky for him, he had already lost his freedom to make that choice. His own life had veered so far from the path he had lived with Mom for all those decades that it almost didn't matter anymore. As far as that goes, part of me felt like it was almost better for her too, this ending. Had Dad actually died in June 2010, it might have been easier on us all. But God and the Universe had a plan, and there was little that any of us could do to alter that plan. We were all on this ride for our own reasons, but it was a ride no less, and the only part we could control was how long we held on.

On the way down from West Pine I called Matt Stimson. He worked as an oncology nurse at the University of Michigan Hospital. He gave me his thoughts on Mom's situation based on all that he had seen like it. I both found it something I could barely listen to and something I knew I had to hear because it contained the steps my life was about to take, and I needed to keep track, write everything down, and remember.

Matt said liver cancer is a painful way to die. People try over and over to cure it through all the ways people typically try to cure cancer. And it works, for a little while. But then inevitably all those beautiful red and white blood cells that course through the human body have to go through the liver, the organ that gathers all the junk out of the blood, and sends it on through, along with the cancer cells. So no matter how hard a person tried, the liver always came back around and ruined everything. It never took more than a year, Matt said. He had never seen anyone make it longer than that.

My next call was to my friend Chad. He's an anesthesiologist at UM. Matt had mentioned when we called UM to ask for an appointment, we should find a doctor to reference, some name we could drop. He was vague, but I got the impression he was saying without a connection to the hospital, without someone who could take my mom's hand and walk her in to a doctor's office, we would never get an appointment in time. We would sit, waiting on a list or on the phone, waiting while the cancer grew, waiting to see if someone could tell us anything different. In the end I think, much like God and the Universe have already decided how things are going to go, if you have a connection to the UM and you get in quickly and you get cured faster, it's only because you were going to live anyway. If God and the Universe have decided it's your time to go, you can get a red carpet leading right up to the CEO of Cancer Cures and you will die, the same death you were going to die, just with fewer appointments in between.

When I called, Chad asked me to read him the notes in Mom's

medical records. We had gotten a copy of the test results from the doctor in West Pine. When I was done, he said he would e-mail someone he knew and would copy me. He fulfilled his promise within an hour of our conversation. Within three hours, my mom had an appointment scheduled with a real cancer specialist at the UM for 9:00 a.m. the next day.

The next morning, we all went to the appointment. I drove my mom's car; we parked in the cancer parking structure next to the building. They made it as easy as possible for people facing what was likely their end. The staff was gracious and understanding, patient. Mom walked in without any assistance from us or the wheelchair they offered her at the door. This would be the only time she made it to a UM appointment on her own two feet. We made our way to the second floor, my mom armed with her insurance cards and a granola bar, a small bottle of water and some juice they offered her after taking her blood. The waiting room was big; there were sick people of all kinds there: young women, old people; children. They called Mom's name. We all followed the nurse, stopping to get her weight in the hallway between the nurses' station and the examination rooms. When she had the procedure in West Pine she had weighed 120 pounds. Now she weighed 110.

We crammed into another small examination room, Grace, Scott, Alex, and Mom. I sat next to Mom on a stool. I felt like the little sister again surrounded by people who were more qualified to help Mom. Why is it that family patterns and roles never seem to leave us? They rear their ugly heads whenever there's a family crisis. My heavy heart of badness was filling up with all those familiar feelings just when the timing was worst. A resident specialist came in the room and asked my mom to sit on the examination table. He observed her as she hopped up on the table and turned around, sitting down. He commented on her strength. She looked like a little girl on display, with all her people watching, all the people who would critique how strong she looked. She refused to show any weakness or fear, but I think I saw a glimmer. I think I saw a little bit of my mom disappearing, even as we sat there. We talked about nutrition, and eating, and how she felt. He asked about the pain in her abdomen. She said there was very little. He asked her what she wanted to do—fight, or be comfortable. She said fight. I felt happy she said that, and I felt afraid of how it would go, what would happened if it failed, and what that would look like. I would do what I could. But I didn't know how this would go. I didn't know how to have anything other than hope. But the hope was not something I could admit out loud to anyone else. I stayed quiet. I said nothing. I prayed.

The doctor made arrangements for Mom to come back on Friday for the port to be put in her chest and to get her first chemotherapy treatment. The port would be how they would pump the chemotherapy drugs in; but there were other things to know and prepare for. This was Wednesday. The port would come Friday. Chemo would come Monday. We were on it now--the bus, the car, the bike, whatever the ride. There was no getting off.

When Mom got sick I was working for a small software company. Two years earlier I had left behind a successful career a few months after Dad had his stroke. I had loved the career I was pursuing, but it was too much work. I couldn't manage the family emergencies and manage my clients at the same time. So I found a less strenuous position with the software company. It was far from challenging and was well beneath my capabilities, but the job was easy. The only downfall was the man I worked for, the CEO. He was a narcissist, abusive and insecure. He thought I drank. He thought I lied about my parents' situation. I learned from a mutual friend his wife was afraid of him. It wouldn't be long before I didn't have to worry about him anyway. He told me shortly after my mom was diagnosed that he was eliminating my position as of March 30, which was about six weeks away. I would soon be without a job at all, but I had bigger things to worry about in the meantime.

22

Independent Living, or Not

When we left UM hospital with the instructions for the upcoming week, we knew there were a lot of decisions to make, the biggest one being where my parents would live. We were entering Week One of Mom's treatment; she would need to be near UM hospital for the foreseeable future. My dad was in West Pine with Jeannie, who was staying with him twenty-four hours a day. Jeannie had resorted to washing the walls at my parents' house to stay busy all day. She was cleaning out the pantry. She was giving the dog daily baths and mopping the floor every time he came in and out the dog door. She had started a new routine with my dad. She would use the hoyer lift to sit him in the blue La-Z-Boy chair in front of the TV, then prop up his feet and give him a bowl of popcorn or peanuts to enjoy while he watched *Jeopardy!*. For the first time in two years he sat in a normal chair, a comfortable chair, a chair with a footrest that went up and took pressure off his back and made him feel like a normal person. When Mom and I walked in the house Friday evening after having driven the two and a half hours from Ann Arbor, seeing him in the blue chair with a bowl of popcorn and *Jeopardy!* on the TV made things seem almost normal for a moment.

We packed some items my mom would need for her time in Ann Arbor. Grace and I would take turns looking after her. She could stay at Grace's house for a few days, and then come to mine. Grace's house seemed more comfortable to me. Her furniture was soft and her couch was perfect for sleeping. She lived alone; Alex was still in North Carolina in their house she had left behind to come up to Michigan. For years since they had gotten married, Grace had thought of leaving Alex. Grace and her first husband had been friends with Alex and his first wife. They had all met at college in MI. When Alex and his wife moved to Greenshore with their two girls, Grace and her first husband moved too, thinking it would somehow help their doomed relationship. It didn't. Sometime after Alex and his wife divorced, Alex moved in with Grace. Melanie and I tried to tell Grace that letting Alex move into her house so soon after her first divorce was only going to result in Grace feeling miserable and unhappy again. But she wanted a relationship. You can't tell people who have made up their minds about love that they are making a mistake. It's the cardinal rule. We tried, and failed, and only years later when Grace called me to say we were right did I feel like I had done the right thing by Grace, or at least tried.

Alex's kids were growing up and getting married and thinking about having babies. They had been at odds with Grace for most of the time she was with Alex because they were teenagers when it all started. To make matters worse, Alex's ex-wife had developed ovarian cancer a couple of years ago and died. After that happened, things seemed to improve and for a while I thought it might all work out for them in Greenshore. But in the months before the stroke, Grace and I talked about how she wanted to move back to Michigan so she didn't miss any more time with Mom and Dad. My dad's stroke was all the excuse Grace needed to move north. She rented a townhouse in Canton that Mom and I tracked down one evening. Grace would rent the townhouse for over two years, with her three cats and her comfy plaid couches and her plants. It was a space that worked well for keeping Mom comfortable, at least until we figured something else out.

Mom and I left Sunday evening and drove back to Ann Arbor with her items. She left my dad with a kiss and a promise to see him in six days, the longest they had ever been apart since they were married in 1958. The house on the forty acres no longer had the feel of a house full of peace and love and history. Now it felt disjointed, half-built, and transitory. It felt very much like something was coming to an end. Jeannie pushed my dad in his wheelchair into the living room and set a small table in front of him. My dad ate his tuna sandwich and chips, drank his water, and watched the news while Daniel ate the crumbs falling from my dad's lap and jumped up waiting for a bite. "He's leaving scratches on your dad's leg," Jeannie said. "He's going to break the skin." I looked down at Daniel's worried little eyes. My dad ate his potato chips absently, sadly. He knew my mom was sick. The anti-depressants he had been on since the stroke kept him numb. He never seemed to spin anymore like he did when he first had the stroke, when his emotions would get stuck or spill out in a tumble, nonsensical like his words. These days he just kept moving forward without much feeling at all. He had nowhere left to go.

We locked the doggy door on the way out so Daniel couldn't

escape. As we drove away, Mom reiterated something she had always told me: she was grateful she never had a mentally challenged child, because she didn't think she could handle it. She didn't have the patience. Even as a child I knew she was right; she didn't have the patience or the compassion to raise a child who was slower or weaker. But we all have our shortcomings. At least she recognized hers in this case. Some of us are lucky enough to understand our shortcomings ahead of time. Some of us learn what those shortcomings are only after we hit that place in ourselves, meet failure and are left stunned, unbelieving.

We stayed at my house in Ann Arbor that night. I would drive Mom to chemo in the morning. I had the paperwork and I needed to be the one to take her, for my own sanity. We went to bed shortly after we got back, but Mom was restless and uncomfortable. Her pain was increasing, and our couch was not a good option for sleeping, so I pulled out the blow-up mattress and helped her lay down. Scott had arrived home late from a trip earlier that day and I didn't want to wake him, so I slept upstairs in the guest bedroom. Our guest room was part of the loft upstairs. We had a vaulted ceiling with a catwalk that led to the bedroom and bathroom. I lied down on top of the covers and even though I usually use a fan for white noise, I didn't that night. I felt like I needed to hear her. Our house was too still and I was out of my element sleeping on the guest bed. I couldn't sleep. On any other night Maia could be found wandering the house at all hours singing—more like screaming--at the top of her lungs her old cat cry. It usually didn't disturb Scott or me much because we had discovered if we closed bedroom door and ran a fan in our room at night, we could drown it out. But alone upstairs, I could hear Maia's wailing and thought it would wake my mom, who I could hear moving restlessly on the mattress downstairs. I whispered sternly to Maia, ordering her to stop. She walked across my chest and lay down on my stomach. I stroked her fur. I was exhausted. I wasn't going to get any sleep like this but there was nothing else to do. I couldn't change what was happening; I could only do as my dad had done when Mom and I left the forty acres earlier that day. Keep moving forward.

23

Pretty Little Poison

My mom was her usual self when Monday rolled around, at least from the outside. I was a mess. We had to leave for the hospital at 6:00 a.m. I drove out of the garage with the folder of her medical records on the roof of my car. Luckily I looked behind me to see papers blowing away from the car and stopped to gather things up before getting out of the neighborhood.

The day was long, starting with the procedure to have the port placed under her skin; then the trip upstairs to talk to the nutritionist for an hour; then sitting in the clinic waiting for blood tests. The Cancer Center had a permanent phlebotomy department fifty feet from the entrance because it had to be done every time a patient came to the center. It was both admirable, their forethought with all of this, and utterly maddening. I wanted them to make the blood draw part like climbing Mt. Everest. I wanted them to make people who had to go there feel like they could do anything--not that they couldn't survive a walk across the carpet that lasted longer than two minutes. And yet, in many cases, that was true. So my indignation was misdirected; it was my own weakness, my own sadness at knowing this situation was the beginning of the end that made me stubborn. I fought the idea. But it wasn't my illness to fight and anyway; fighting cancer was already exactly like climbing Mt. Everest.

We navigated her appointments like it was our job. And in a lot of ways, I guess it was. Mom had made it her job to take care of Dad in every way after his stroke. I made it my job to take care of her. I got good at finding her magazines and talking to pharmacists about pills. Mom didn't swallow pills easily, so we needed liquid prescriptions whenever we could get them. We had a bad choking incident when Mom was at my house, and I realized after that we had to be extra careful. I wanted to think of every little detail. I wanted to be the one who solved all the problems before they came up. If I could have carried her on my back, I would have. But my heavy heart of badness kept reminding me no matter what, I would never be able to do enough.

Her first chemo treatment started at 1:00 p.m. on Monday. The chairs were comfy and there were lots of people in there doing the same thing. First, they pumped her full of a whole liquid bag of vitamins. That's how chemo treatments start. Then they put the poison bag up and hooked it to her port. We had been warned she would feel great the first few hours after chemo because of the vitamins. Then the chemo drugs would kick in. Life would get much worse for a few days; then things would improve. We would repeat this process every ten days or so until something changed. The cancer would get better or it would get worse, but it would change, and then life would change again. We nodded our heads at this. We got it. We understood.

As advertised, the first few hours after chemo Mom felt great. Great is a relative term for a woman who was seventy-four years old and had metastatic liver disease. She could get in and out of the car with minimal help. She ate a little something when we stopped at Panera on the way home. We made a comfy spot for her on the couch. She would go back to my sister's the next day. The chemo was taking over already; I gave her my bed to sleep in and she couldn't get up in it without a boost. I worried about her falling out, so I slept fitfully on the couch. I woke with a start at 3:00 a.m. when she got up to go to the bathroom. I ran in so quickly from the living room I startled her. She laughed. I helped her to the commode. I helped her sit down. I never realized how far down a toilet can be for someone who has no strength; she held on to the door knob like a little child, her pants caught up around her knees, grasping and stretching with both hands around the knob hoping it would help her to sit and feel safe. I was there to catch her if she fell.

We showered her the next morning before my sister came to pick her up. I was late for work again. I didn't care. It didn't matter to me if the crazy CEO thought I drank and lied about my parents. My mom was dying. She told me not to look at her as we pulled off her sweatshirt; she was so thin. I promised not to look. She was afraid of the slippery shower floor, so I used a technique Scott told me they teach pilots in training school—put a towel on the floor of the shower to avoid slipping. Many a pilot has apparently not made it to the hotel bus heading for the airport after he slips on the shower floor and hits his head on the tub. I thought it was ingenious. She laughed. It worked, though, she felt steadier with the towel to stand on. I helped her sit down on the shower enclosure seat and shampooed her hair with my favorite shampoo, mint and eucalyptus. I let the water run over her back and shoulders.

I never had been good at living in the moment and when I was younger I often thought greener grass grew always somewhere further west. I searched for the better situation and never stopped moving. Somehow I found myself so much more present in these days. I needed every moment saved on a permanent disk in my brain, to play over and over: her soft hair, her thin frame, her voice. For my whole life after this I would need to take all the moments I had heard her laugh and talk and I would have to remember them as they were, because more than half of my life would now be spent without ever hearing them again.

24

Empty, Or How I Felt

race called me Tuesday night, thirty-six hours after chemo. I had driven Mom over to Grace's that morning and
spent the day with her. She slept for most of it. I spent the day making phone calls to do things like cancel the cable and the phone at
the forty acres. I argued with every customer service department.
They wanted to talk to Mom to be sure this was for real. Part of
me understood they were doing this to protect their customers, following a protocol for cancelling accounts. But another part of me
was angry. At one point after going in circles, I finally said to the
customer service agent, "You can't talk to her because she's dead." I
hoped Mom was sleeping and didn't hear. As the afternoon wore on,
I realized she wasn't hearing much. She was practically comatose
with sleep. I phoned the doctor. "That's normal," he said. "She will
be more alert soon." I left as soon as Grace got home from work,
eager to do something normal.

But that didn't last long. Grace called within two hours of my leaving. "Mom tried to stand up from the couch by herself and ended up sliding back down to the floor," Grace said. "Now I can't get her up."

"Do you want me to come over?" I asked.

"No," Grace said.

She thought she could figure something out. I could hear Mom in the background, like a petulant child or a drunk person lying in the street, complaining loudly about why did she have to get up off the floor? Why couldn't she just stay here? Grace's laugh was bordering on hysterical. She was standing in the kitchen where Mom couldn't see her.

"She's acting weird," Grace said. "She's arguing she doesn't need to get up, like I'm being unreasonable." Mom was on the floor, her nightgown around her waist, her hair a mess, looking blank-eyed and barely able to sit up, and yet saw nothing wrong with it.

I told Grace to call me if she needed help. I felt weary from the constant helping and I know Grace did too. For two grown women who have no children, sometimes it seemed like we weren't cut out for it, all this caregiving. Like we had we already gone through all our reserves. Sometimes it felt like we should be able to call a truce, but with whom?

The next morning I call around to a few places and found an apartment at an independent living facility that had one handicapped unit available. We could move my parents in the next weekend. The stress of their healthcare expenses was back to weighing on us. The Davis house situation had cost thousands a month between the rented temporary wheelchair ramp, the cost of utilities, the rental amount I secretly gave Matt and Lee for the use of the space, but mostly the 24/7 caregivers. My parents ran through all of their savings in four months. Once they moved home, though, my mom didn't hire much in the way of extra help, both to save money and because it was her home, her space. In the end, all of the stress put on her had undoubtedly sped up the inevitable with regard to her cancer diagnosis. No doubt her illness was there long before the stroke, but in a matter of less than a year, it grew up into a full-blown disease that was devouring her, body and mind.

The new apartment was in between Ann Arbor and Ypsilanti on a busy main artery that had nice enough amenities within walking distance. It backed up to a bit of woods and had a pond with ducks. We soon learned a feral cat colony lived in the woods behind the apartment complex and ate from the dumpster not far from my parents' patio door. The cats were of all sizes and ages. An old woman who lived on the third floor left bread and other food scraps for them. I went to see the apartment and talked to Beverly, the woman in charge of running the complex. It catered to veterans, so there were lots of old men gathered in the common room just inside the front door. I hadn't yet grown used to the idea that my parents no longer were independent people and couldn't live in the home they had created together--the dignified, warm, familiar space we all had known with the flower beds and the maple trees and the well-groomed yard. Beverly showed me the apartment, pointing out several times how serendipitous it was that they had a first-floor handicapped apartment available right now, and what did I think of it? They would paint and clean the carpets before we got there next weekend. I wandered around the generic space thinking it reminded me of the last apartment my grandparents lived in before my grandmother died. It was the same Berber carpet, dull white walls, and cheap cabinets with one dim overhead light above the dining area. I hated everything about it. I hated what it represented and how it made me feel and the direction it was taking our world.

I turned to Beverly. "It's perfect, we'll take it."

We arranged to move them that weekend from West Pine to the apartment. Jeannie was willing to stay with my dad until then. We had never known her before she started working for my parents, but she of course knew many of the same people my parents knew because West Pine is a small town and my parents were a well-known fixture. Dad taught high school math for thirty years before retiring in 1994. My mother had worked for various medical facilities in town and as a secretary for a law firm during my growing up years. Jeannie fielded the many questions, phone calls and cards that came in the mail while we were all away from the forty acres and it was just her, Daniel, and my dad. My mom attempted to respond to each card and phone call by herself at first, then grew unable to keep up with the barrage, and then grew unable to open the mail or remember how to use her cell phone. Soon she would grow too weak and sore to speak, her mouth full of thrush--a byproduct of chemotherapy.

Alex, Scott, and I went up to West Pine Saturday morning with a moving truck. We packed a smattering of furniture and dishes and clothing into the truck. Alex would drive it back down to Ann Arbor. Scott and I left West Pine before lunchtime in my parents' car with my dad in the passenger's seat. Scott kept my dad busy asking questions and letting Dad take his time telling us the answers. Dad enjoyed the normalcy of the conversation and the drive. We stopped at YaYa's, a take-out chicken shop that had sandwiches and baked beans, and was food we could eat in the car. My dad ate with relish. He seemed to be thinking for a moment of something other than my mother, or his stroke, or everything he had lost and was about to lose. We had told him they would be living in Ann Arbor while my mom was sick, and then we could move them back to West Pine after the chemo. I didn't know then how much of this my dad understood, but looking back I know he understood much more than we suspected. He may not have been able to speak the words or thoughts or ideas or dreams or fears he felt, but those fears rattled around in his heavy heart, just like they did in mine.

Grace stayed in Canton with my mom while we moved their things from West Pine to the new apartment. It had been six days since the first chemo treatment, and Mom was due to go back to the doctor on Monday. She was still weak and sick, looking less like herself all the time. My sister had helped Mom up to the second floor of her townhouse so Mom could take a bath, which apparently hadn't gone particularly well. Grace and Mom were not getting along very well. Grace's patience ran along the same lines as Melanie's and my dad's. None of them had the ability to hold their tempers or be rational when situations got particularly tough. I had grown up seeing it. I had grown up hearing my sisters argue about how our family didn't ever talk about anything, how we hid behind our issues, how we never were honest with our feelings. Even then I wondered why being honest with feelings had to mean screaming and throwing stuff. Maybe my idea of being honest with feelings was different from theirs, but I thought it made more sense to be reasonable than to dump every angry emotion you had on the person sitting closest to you who happened to share some genes. But that opinion seemed to stop with my mom and me when it came to the family circle. My mom rarely lost her temper but could be incredibly two-faced. My dad had a terrible temper, but I rarely heard him say an unkind word about someone. I wanted to be a person who didn't lose her temper and didn't talk unkindly about people. But I was pretty sure that was a level of perfection my heavy heart could not attain. I would both lose my temper and talk about people, I was certain. But I would try hard not to.

Grace kept my mom at her house until we got the moving truck down to the apartment and the few of our friends who stopped by to help unload it were gone. It took only a few minutes and then we were left to unpack. Grace didn't think our friends should see Mom in the condition she was in and I agreed. Most of these people had known her for most of my life, or at least for enough years to make it hard on everyone if they did see her. After my sister and Mom arrived and we got her in the door and resting comfortably on the couch, we started to unpack. The important things came first: my mom's coffee pot, her robe, their TV, Dad's blue chair. We hung pictures and made it homey. There were two bedrooms, so they each had plenty of space. I went to Target and bought Mom a memory foam pad for her mattress. By now she was so thin her tail bone stuck out, so lying on a regular mattress was painful. As we settled in I could see she was uncomfortable in her wheelchair. I wondered what I could get for her other than a pillow or a chair pad to make it more tolerable. I went out and spent money on any random item I thought would help, buying comfort with dollars and willing to do whatever it took. I would have run into the middle of the busy inter-section in front of their apartment to die if I thought it would make a difference. I would have stolen, I would have lied. I was desperate.

25

It's All Kinds of Bad

om's doctor watched her closely Monday morning when we arrived. This time she was visibly weak and unable to get up on the examining table at all. She couldn't walk without help; she couldn't get up from her wheelchair without the nurse's assistance. She was dying. I tried not to notice it and really, it wasn't until later looking back I realize how obvious it was. But hindsight is always clearer, and not knowing when the end would come meant it was easier to look past what was there in front of me. None of it seemed particularly real--it was just a hurtling train we were on; it was just the journey, like pulling into a car wash and lining up your car tires with the grooves so you could throw it into neutral and let the belts pull you through. When we had first met with the doctor exactly fourteen days ago, he had asked my mom what she wanted, and she said she wanted to fight. One round of chemo and five doctor's appointments later, it was clear even to me she couldn't go through that again. The very idea of it meant we would be killing her.

I had called the doctor when she was in the midst of the first week after chemo for advice on what to expect and what we should be looking for, even though we had already heard it before. I'm not sure what doctors learn in medical school about telling their patients and the families when the end is near. I imagine it's as difficult for doctors to talk about it as it is for anyone else. Maybe it's even harder because they have seen it before and they know what's coming. I think if I were a doctor I would grow weary of being delicate, of giving patients the chance to follow their unrealistic courses of action and encouraging results I know will never materialize. Though Matt Stimson's words to me three weeks earlier had been forthright and harsh, it was the only thing I had heard from anyone about this situation that had provided direction, legitimacy--a twelve-step program toward truth and reality.

Mom's doctor told us while we sat there that Mom couldn't manage chemo again. He suggested other ways to manage her illness more naturally. She could continue to fight it with good nutrition and vitamins and medication to manage her pain. In other words, her journey was ending, soon. The Institution that was the UM Hospital was officially done helping us, because we were beyond their help. We should call hospice. He gave us the hospice pep talk. Hospice doesn't just help people who are at the ends of their lives, but it helps people to live with quality for the rest of the time they live, whatever that means. He was right about all of it; I knew that. But I also knew from Mom's body language that this was the twelfth step in the program as far as she was concerned.

I was the only one with Mom at that last appointment with the doctor at UM. She was coughing an aggravated cough that left her on the verge of gagging. She was behaving like she was drunk. The doctor told us she was dehydrated. He instructed me to take her to the area where she had received chemo and the staff could give her an infusion of vitamins and fluids. When we got her hooked up to the IV fluids, I started to realize we were close to the end. The nurses were acting nice, but kept their distance. They didn't spend time making a connection like they had before when we were here for chemo. I felt sad and embarrassed and ashamed, I didn't know why. It's like she had used up her goodwill to be here. I wanted them to still treat her like she was a champion, a warrior. I wanted us to still be in the group of the living.

We stopped for lunch on the way home. Mom wanted to get a newspaper, a normal activity in her life. She had traveled into town every day to pick up a paper once the *West Pine Herald* no longer delivered to my parents' house. When they lived in the Davis house, she would pick up a *USA Today* on the way to see my dad, and subscribed to the Sunday edition of the *Ann Arbor News*. She had recently begun to do things that were routine for her, but then not follow through as if she lost her train of thought. She would get up early each morning at the apartment to make coffee before the caregivers arrived, but then would forget to drink it. My mother loved her morning coffee and would pour several cups during the course of the morning every day of my life, sipping them until they grew cold. It was a family joke. We could tell which coffee cup belonged to my mom and which to my dad, because my mom's always had a little dribble down the outside of her cup. I must have inherited this trait from her; my cups have the same coffee dribble marks.

Mom insisted on getting a hamburger for my dad since it would be lunchtime for him when we arrived back at the apartment, so we stopped to buy a hamburger at the McDonalds on Plymouth Rd and get a newspaper at the gas station next door. She didn't have to worry about feeding him anymore, but old habits die hard. In West Pine Mom was able to look after Dad for the most part, with some help from Jeannie, until everything started to fall apart. Now that they were back in Ann Arbor, they could be left alone at night in their separate rooms to sleep but needed someone there during the day. I had called the agency we used when they were at the Davis house earlier that day, and by the time Mom and I got back to the apartment, a young woman named Erika was there waiting for us. She would take care of my dad and keep an eye on my mom from early morning until bedtime. Our first order of business was to call hospice and set up an appointment to have them come over and talk to Mom. They could be there within a couple of hours. Mom didn't argue with the arrangements, but I could see her demeanor was shifting. The hospice nurse came, talked to Mom and left specific instructions with some narcotics for pain. She was all done and had left by 5:00 p.m.

After they moved to the independent living apartment, Mom and Dad refused to go down to the cafeteria to eat. It was as if they didn't want to meet anyone new because it would require talking, something too painful for Mom and nearly impossible for Dad. Erika went down to get food trays for them and brought them back. They sat at the table together in their wheelchairs, defeated, like some kind of picture I didn't recognize. They were marriage partners for fifty-two years, brought together by chance in college and kept together through all the trials of married life with children. They had always been a team. My whole life I thought of them that way, and when the stroke came to take over our family I saw my mom was left in the lead role alone where there had always been two. It was too much for her by then, too much with all the history, and their dreams, and her growing illness. Now they were together in a place neither of them would have chosen, brought there by circumstance, time, illness, age, and soon death. They sat together at the table picking at the food on their trays and waiting for the end to come.

Her last doctor's appointment was on Monday. By Tuesday evening Mom was barely getting up from the couch. Erika was a godsend. Grace and I could carry on with our daily lives, as much as we could in light of the situation. On Wednesday morning my sister called me at work. We talked about Mom's death. We had been sisters all our lives, but as adults we had spent very little time together. We saw each other at Christmas for the last fifteen years; that was pretty much it. We knew the basics. I knew she drove me nuts if I spent too much time with her. I figured she felt the same about me. I knew she went to church; we were both raised in the Methodist Church, attending Sunday school and summer Bible camp. Her first and second husbands were both Baptist. Mom and I talked occasionally about Grace's political leanings, her second husband, but Mom never said negative things about Grace to me, and I suspected she did the same with Grace when it came to me. Mom could be petty, she could be two-faced; she could be things I never saw in her until Dad got sick, and even worse, when she got sick. But I can chalk those up to the worst moments for anyone. I want to think I would do better, but I can't judge. I don't know. But one thing Mom didn't do was badmouth my dad in front of me, or my sister. She was loyal to us, to all of us together and individually.

26

When It's Over

The manager of the home health company, Christine, called me at work on Wednesday just before lunch. "Erika is having trouble getting your mother off the couch," she said. "I'm going over there to help her." I was confused. Why would Christine call to tell me this? Did Erika need a hand with my mom? If so, she could have called me. Erika and I had become something like friends beyond just the work she was doing for us. Our lives were very different, but she was smart and worked hard and I trusted her. She had her medical assistant certification. She was smaller than average in stature, but she was strong and certainly capable of getting my mom up off the couch by herself. Doctor visits showed Mom weighed less than 100 pounds now. My first thought was that Erika had hurt herself and now we'd have to find someone else to help. I felt a pang of irritation, impatience, exhaustion, followed by guilt for feeling all of this. I didn't have the energy left to worry about training someone else. The overused metaphor in my head told me our lives were like a car wash—you drive in, car wheels in the wells, directions on the blinking sign—put it in neutral, no hands on the wheel. We were moving without any control, being pulled along, and I just didn't have the strength to fight anymore.

I don't remember exactly what else Christine said, but I remember being very confused by her words. I just wanted her to say something that made sense. I repeated what she said about Erika and my mom. Christine paused. She was going to go over and help Erika get my mom into bed. "Okay, and then what?" I asked.

"You should call hospice," she said. "You should let them know."

"Let them know what? That Erika needs help?" Then I understood. My mom was going to lie down in her bed, with the help of Erika and Christine, for what was likely the last time in her life. "Okay," I told her, "I'll call the nurse." I hung up.

Hospice came right away, only forty-eight hours since they first came with their pamphlets and medications and supportive words. They told us it would be another few days, a week perhaps. They would bring the hospital bed, the mattress with the little pillows that inflate and deflate; my dad had one of those too. I was used to the hissing noise it made and the hum of the attached pump. They would bring the oxygen tank to be used as needed. They told us to be careful with a full oxygen tank in the apartment. There were things we needed to know. I was only partly listening.

We had caregivers around the clock now, for the foreseeable future. The caregivers were all friendly. They seemed to care. I wondered how they could care this much for people they didn't know-- people in this condition, people who needed them to do the things we needed them to do, but who were not their own family members. They didn't get paid enough to make it worth their while.

Before long we realized one of them was stealing from us--Xavier. My headphones had disappeared along with some of our wipes, and then shortly thereafter, some of Mom's hospice meds. Erika surmised he was taking things to sell. Mom lay in the hospital bed in her room, her mouth gaping open as she breathed in and out. We moved the full sized bed from her room into the living room and moved the loveseat in across from her hospital bed. The caregivers could sleep on the mattress in the living room if they needed rest. Because as of now, someone had to be there twenty-four hours a day until she died.

Grace and I continued to work. I was going to be out of a job in two days, my crazy boss having laid me off as of March 30. I hardly thought about work. I hardly cared about work. I had nothing to do at work, really, since he hated me for whatever reason and hadn't looked at or spoken to me for the last two months of my employment. I had another good friend at work and we made use of the time. I helped her with the upcoming taxes for the business; she asked questions about my parents. She was sympathetic and compassionate and would tear up about many things that happened. She would be a friend of mine long after I left the job--the only good thing that came from it, like so many things in life. There is always at least one thing to take away from any bad situation in life: one thing to learn from, to treasure, no matter what it was. I had learned that quickly in life, starting with Shane and the Mother's Day adventure. I had tried to find the lessons in what Melanie brought to my life, our lives; there was good in all of us, no matter how difficult we all made it for each other. Grace had called Melanie and told her about Mom, that the end was coming soon. Melanie asked why we had not told her sooner, that we must be enjoying spending all this time together, caring for them.

"Oh yes," Grace said. "It's great. This experience is something we certainly are enjoying so much we wouldn't possibly want to share it with anyone else. But if you want to see Mom, you should come soon."

The nurse checked in again Thursday morning. Mom was still on her back, her mouth open, breathing deeply. The nurse left toothettes—they looked like little pink spongy lollipops. She instructed us to wet them and swab Mom's mouth to keep it moist. Erika changed Mom's brief. We had never officially asked the agency to have Erika watch Mom along with Dad, but she did it anyway. She helped wherever she was needed, without question. Erika sat on the loveseat we had moved into Mom's room whenever Dad was napping in his own bed. Grace and I were torn. Should we be sitting with Mom too? Hospice thought it could be a few days to a week before she passed. We were paying Erika to be there, to care for them while we worked; we trusted her implicitly. So much of our lives had been changed and interrupted and ended, so much of it feeling and being out of our control. We had learned from the stroke that things can be bad but life went on, relentlessly, unforgiving; the new normal. This was different. We were not prepared for changes that took away the normal entirely and replaced it with nothing. Just snuffed out what was known and left us empty.

So Grace and I agreed we should do what we were doing and keep up with normal life as much as possible. After all, Mom would want us to do that and we would have some kind of warning when things were nearing the very end. Mom was not the kind of person who would want us sitting with her, doing nothing, staring, as her mouth hung open and skeletal across her thin face. She was not our mom anymore. I visited them Thursday evening. Dad was already in bed, depressed. Erika said she took Dad in each night to kiss Mom good night. Dad had said good night to Mom shortly before I arrived, Erika said. He told her it was okay to go. "Cleo, Cleo, Cleo," he cried. "It's okay."

On Friday morning, the phone rang at 7:20 a.m., just as I was getting out of the shower. It was Erika. "She's gone."

"I'm on my way," I said.

It was rainy, gray; March 30. It was the last day of my job, and the last day of my mother's life. I texted Scott; he would be home later that day from his trip. I talked to Grace; she would head over to the apartment after she called the cremation service. I drove aimlessly toward their apartment, feeling the need to tell someone, to call someone. Someone else in Mom's life should know. There were people I should call to share this news. There were so many who would want to know, but I wanted to tell someone in particular. I reached for my wallet. Alice's number was in there. Alice, my mom's best friend, was in her 80s now. Even though I had just called Alice a few weeks ago when Mom had her procedure, I hadn't actually seen Alice in fifteen years. Still her face was with me, her face I knew from thirty years ago. She answered.

"I just wanted to let you know that Mom died today."

"Okay," she said.

"She always told me you were her best friend," I said. I started to cry.

"Thank you," she said. She was crying too. "Goodbye."

We hung up. I felt strange after the awkward, short conversation. I probably shouldn't have called after all, I realized. *I am acting hysterical, I can't talk to people about this; I shouldn't have called her.* I think about that call sometimes still. Because every week Alice sends Dad a letter just like she did for Mom, even now.

My sister arrived at the apartment the same time I did. Erika had alerted Barbara at the front office. She brought us breakfast items from the cafeteria and gave her condolences. My dad was inconsolable, reticent. It was hard enough for him to communicate on a good day. Now he had no words to say; he just cried. I glanced at my mom when I walked by her room, lying on the hospital bed, still. I wanted to go in to see her, to say goodbye but somewhere something inside of me I hesitated. There was nothing left of the woman who was my mother anymore. Her body was there, but her journey here was over. She had moved on to the next part of her existence, without us. I didn't feel her with us then, but I felt sure I would again soon. We had talked about that before, about how we felt Grandma after she died, about how we sensed things. I knew she would come to me, somehow. But I couldn't worry about that now. I couldn't listen for her yet. Right now we had to take care of the details of death.

The crematorium sent a short gentleman in a suit to pick up Mom, a plastic flower in his lapel. He explained the details to us. Mom and Dad had paid for their cremation already; we simply needed to let them know and they would take care of the rest. He went about his business in Mom's room while we gathered in the living room, talking amongst ourselves, Erika, Grace, Christine, Barbara, and me. It was nearly lunchtime by now, and Erika went down to get my dad's lunch, a hamburger. I put the tray on his lap, hesitant to engage with him in front of everyone. Hesitant because none of us were crying, but we were all on the verge, we all needed to. Grace and I were exhibiting our mother's strongest quality, calm in a storm. Erika cut Dad's hamburger in quarters. He ate it because it was there, and sobbed.

27

To Rest

race and I went up to West Pine in early June just before Grace's birthday. Our birthdays were exactly three weeks apart—mine first, then hers. Father's Day was always close behind. After Mom died, we knew Dad would not go home to the forty acres again. Dad knew that too, but we didn't talk about it. He was living alone now in the apartment, with Erika and a couple of other care-givers coming in every day from 7:00 a.m. to 7:00 p.m. They would get him up for breakfast when they arrived and put him to bed when they left, and he would remain there, alone, through the night with a single check-in by the patient care group that had an office in the complex. The inpatient care group at the apartment complex was unreliable at best, and between the rent and the cost of home health care, this wasn't a long-term solution. We hoped and dreamed Dad would make friends there and have some kind of life, perhaps enjoy-ing some friendship over a game of Hearts, or Bingo, or even just a daily visitor, someone who enjoyed him the way people always had enjoyed his friendship before the stroke. But Erika was his only companion. She finally convinced Dad to go to the dining room to eat, and the front office paired him with a group of other vets so they could all eat together.

Dad's ability to carry on a meaningful conversation was gone, but he wasn't the only stroke victim who ate at that table. He would need to learn to not only overcome his aphasia, but also live without having his Cleo, Cleo, Cleo. Dad didn't like to leave the apartment other than for the occasional stroll around the pond, or a special occasion when we would go to the "modern Coney Island" in the strip mall next door to the apartment complex. He was depressed, but it was managed with the medication he had been taking since the stroke. I would sometimes imagine what we would have had in store had my father not become the invalid long before my mother did. My father was minimally suicidal in his thoughts and behavior starting around the time he had prostate cancer. That would have been sometime in the early 2000s.

It was my first stint living in Flagstaff, Arizona and I was dirt poor. I had moved out there with less than $500 in my pocket and it took a couple of weeks to find a job. I was gainfully employed when my dad got sick, but not the kind of employed that afforded me a plane ticket to Detroit for several hundred dollars. A Greyhound bus ticket, however, was $69 round trip. I only had to be on the bus for forty-eight hours straight if I wanted to get to Bay City, Michigan. *No problem*, I thought. *I can do that.* I like to remember that time as complete freedom, but it's hard to remember if I just look back at it that way, or if I really felt that way. When I first moved to Arizona I felt like I was on vacation every day. Even after I took a job that didn't match my education or skill level, I found friends and new places to explore. I was less lonely as time passed; I spent fewer and fewer nights wishing it wasn't the weekend for so many hours between Friday afternoon and Monday morning. Soon I met a new boy, and as always I felt my freedom drift away and be replaced by the gray clouds of relationships that sometimes rained on me, and sometimes showed the sun, but my trailing atmosphere was nothing if not confusing to me. I sought out love all the time—I wanted a boyfriend--but was never happy when I had one. On the Greyhound bus riding home to see my parents, I felt the lightness in my heavy heart growing lighter and lighter, the further I got from Arizona. I wrote poems about my failures, and my future, and my dreams. I wrote them all in a little notebook covered with camouflage cloth, as if my thoughts needed hiding any more than I already hid them. Maybe Arizona wasn't right for me after all.

I made it home on the bus, and my dad had his surgery, and I went back to Arizona by airplane—a gift from my friend Jen, whose mother had died of ovarian cancer very suddenly only months earlier. Jen traveled for work and had lots of frequent flyer miles; she understood a sick parent situation. She didn't want me to ride the bus all the way back to Flagstaff, and I didn't want to either. I was grateful for the one-way ticket to Phoenix. I think of her gesture often, even to this day. Not long after that happened I moved back to Michigan for a new job—it may have even been just later that year, around Christmas. I didn't want to be away from my parents like that; it was too far. And I knew my dad was depressed. My mom worried about him--she said he had a shotgun hanging in the basement and he would use it someday, she knew he would. He told her he didn't want to get old, that he would rather kill himself than live with his body falling apart.

The winter after I moved to Arizona he had broken his heel

when he slipped off the back of a truck gathering wood with his oldest brother, Mick, who was in his 80s at the time. Dad's foot would never bend quite the same again, and he walked with a limp. Each of these events that took him closer to old age and further from the vitality of youth made him frustrated and angry. But there was no telling him, just like there's no telling any of us that he should be treasuring every moment of his life because things could always be much worse. Things would be much worse for him very soon. And much like God and the Universe home in on the one thing any of us are most afraid of and then plunge us into the depths of that fear so we can do nothing else but face it, so they did to my dad and to the whole family. I had experienced this phenomenon a few times in my life, these lessons and curses imparted by God and the Universe. Had I been astute enough, I would have realized it was bound to happen. My dad was so angry about everything back then. He was angry about his weak foot. He was angry at the results of his prostate cancer and surgery. Had he known what was in store, I am certain he would have been grateful for every moment he had on the forty acres, doing exactly what he wanted to do. My dad and I talk a lot now, reminding ourselves how lucky we are to have warm beds to sleep in, food to eat, and people who love us. I tell him these things to remind him, as much as to remind me.

The day Grace and I drove to West Pine and took my mother's ashes along with Samantha's, we took the long route, just to enjoy one of the last few drives we would ever make up to the house. We drove up the long driveway leading to the forty acres. It looked so alone, the house. Mom's flower beds were overgrown with the beauty of late spring, blossoming and crawling over themselves to reach the sun, to be seen. We had hired a company to cut the grass. Seeing the perfect rows in the lawn almost made me think I heard my dad's tractor as we drove up. I waited to see him round the pole barn, riding the lawn mower. Until we walked to the back of the house and I saw the fruit trees in the little grove, a fence surrounding them to keep out the deer. The grass in the fence was waist-high-- an oversight by those who were caring for the grass. My dad would never have allowed this, and so I came back to our reality. There was no semblance of love here now, only a careless effort made by the landscaping company. The property was otherwise rampant with neglect.

We walked with the ashes to the meadow behind the stand of birch and oak trees near the little swamp where I used to play all those years, alone. So many, many days of my young life spent wandering that meadow, that woods, through all those trees telling stories to myself, to my audience of one. I could recall specific days in my mind, specific places I had wandered in circles talking to myself. Even the seasons came back to me: summer sand between my toes, winter coats with feet of snow, naked branches in spring, early fall with wild brambles and sumac higher than my head.

We walked to my mother's favorite part of the property and stopped. The slight incline of the ground surrounded by spring flowers and warm sun and budding branches was the perfect location for a house, and the spot where they had first thought to build on the forty acres. But it was too close to the property edge and therefore any potential neighbors. They wanted more privacy. So they opted to put the house smack dab in the middle of the land, and Mom just visited the meadow when she wanted peace. In all my life, I remember her going out there only a handful of times. But still we all knew the story; we knew it was her favorite spot. Both Grace and I knew that's where her ashes would go. We opened the boxes, Mom's and Samantha's. We pulled out the plastic bags and each started to spread our respective ashes, walking and talking as we went. After a few minutes we switched so we could both spread a little of each. We agreed when Dad died we would have to come back here, even if the property were owned by someone else then, even if it were the dark of night, to spread his ashes in the meadow too. It would be only right that they should all be here together.

28

Rising

The October after Mom died, we moved Dad out of the independent living apartment and into an assisted living facility. It was another move, another change, another now-familiar place we left behind for the unknown. It was a continuation of life since the day we first went to St. Mary's in Saginaw that mid-June day, taking an exit off the freeway we had never taken before to see streets near downtown Saginaw we had never seen: dilapidated houses, kids in summertime clothes wandering down the sidewalk and loitering on their neighbor's front porch. No restaurants or grocery stores or feelings of home, just unfamiliar streets in places we didn't want to be. Since then we had lived a thousand stories--some with happy endings, others without.

By now our expectations were low. We didn't expect Dad to make friends, or be social, or have a life of any kind. We just wanted him to be dry, fed, and in bed when he wanted to be. We tried at first to instill some of the normalcies of his previous world—toast with strawberry jam for breakfast, showers every other day, bedtime at 7:30 p.m. But we soon discovered this wasn't feasible. Our vision of his life there drew a picture in our minds of caregivers watching over his every need, giving him the things he wanted when he wanted them. But in reality it meant we had to watch him more closely than ever.

Things would disappear from his room: towels, clothing, and other personal items we bought for him. Every time something came up missing it felt like a violation, but of the strangest variety; it wasn't for lack of caring by the staff--it seemed more out of desperation. One time a bath towel and a whole bottle of shampoo disappeared. I imagined they stole in order to take care of the woman in the next room who hadn't showered in weeks and whose daughter was coming to visit, even though I could never get to the bottom of it. I imagined the daughter of the resident contacting the nursing staff demanding her mother be clean when she arrived with family. The resident would cry when the caregivers came to give her a shower because she's old and thin and the water temperature is only ever tepid; this I know from showering my own father. She doesn't want to feel colder than she already does, to have her hands feel numb and immovable, to shiver, to not feel warm again for days after because her bones are so close to the top of her skin and she can't get warm, can never get warm. So the caregivers desperately search her closet for towels and shampoo while she cries and resists. They try to woo her with stories and cajole her toward her bathroom door and all the while they search and there is no towel, no towel in her belongings, because if she had a towel it has long since disappeared with someone else's laundry, or perhaps she never had a towel.

So the caregivers ponder where can they find a clean towel,

something soft and thick that smells clean and homey and might help get this situation moving? They think of my dad, of his cinnamon-scented room from the plug-in air freshener we bought him. They think of his fleece sheets and flannel pants and long-sleeved shirts, always folded neatly in his closet. And his towels, big and fluffy enough to cover this tiny resident completely, to wrap her in softness and warmth so perhaps she will stop crying, and they shower her and move on to the next patient before her daughter arrives. The caregivers have already gone past their allotted time with this resident per the schedule they were given this morning, and they will have to answer to management as to why it has taken them so long. The head of the care staff will ask where these two have been, these two young caregivers in their twenties. She will think they must have been hiding and having a smoke. The caregivers feel the injustice of it on their backs before it even happens. They are afraid of getting in trouble, but they are more afraid of not showering the resident because they know this daughter, and she will complain loudly, and they will hear about it either way. This is why things disappear from Dad's room.

It has been three years now since Mom died. Grace moved back to Greenshore almost two years ago and comes up to visit for a few days every couple of months. We hired Erika away from the agency; she and I take turns looking after Dad at the assisted living facility. We read to him at night: non-fiction, mostly history, some sports. Reading and showering are the activities he most looks forward to each day. Fresh fruit, especially cantaloupe, is a favorite; and a Snickers bar, always the fun size variety, cut in four pieces so he can chew with his few remaining teeth. I have taken to cutting his hair myself every few weeks. I trim his nails, shave his face. It would be nice if we could visit randomly, but I can't bring myself to leave his nighttime routine to anyone else but Erika or me. So each night there is someone with him, someone who can be there at 5:00 p.m. to change his sheets, make the bed; someone to wipe up the counters and replace the dirty hand towel and washcloth in his bathroom. Someone to sweep away the leftover peas from lunchtime that fell from his lap when he stood at the grab bar, grasping tightly with his one functioning hand while someone wipes him clean.

This is his life—it is our life. It is the life that repeats, each day, the same. It is as far from their future as my parents could have imagined, because their discussions never envisioned him like this. Sometimes in my life I have feared things, things mostly related to loss, lack of control, or confrontation. I feared losing my parents. I feared losing Cerin. These were my greatest fears and were events I did not believe I would know how to survive. So God and the Universe took my greatest fears and plunged me into them like a dunk tank. Instantaneous and total immersion—like some kind of horrifying amusement park ride, we went from 0 to 100mph in under a second. And yet, somehow I made it through. I lived. I learned. I survived.

29

The Blessing

mostly forget what it was like to be around Dad before the stroke. I think sometimes I also forget to be grateful for how it turned out; and by that I mean if the fates were going to give me my dad as a man who no longer has control over most of his life, at least they made him sweet, and patient, and forgiving. If the Universe meant to take my mom away quickly from a partnership my parents seemed to treasure now that they had made it through the early married years, the poor years, the hard years with Melanie, the years of boredom and redundancy, to reach the time when they could have their own Samantha puppy to love, their own motorhome to travel in, their early mornings of coffee and chocolate twisty donuts covered in peanuts, it had done her justice by taking her without a lot of drama.

My parents left behind friends who played cards and had costume parties. Friends who married late in life and had a little girl named Amanda who loved horses and called my parents Grandma and Grandpa, the closest they ever came to having a grandchild. If God and the Universe in all their powers meant to take Dad's world away like they did, so fast and with no warning, then they did us all a favor by rendering him a man who could never again get to the loaded shotgun hanging in the basement. Surely God and the Universe talked one day, and what they came up with was the best solution for everyone. They each had a list of lessons we all needed to learn, fears we needed to overcome, paths we needed to take. But they had quite a few members of the Elliott family to work with all at once. I can't purport to have any idea of the deepest fears and needs my family, these people I love so dearly, had in their heavy hearts of badness. I know the paths we took only because of what I see, but I don't really know what my father held inside his self-defeating heart or my mother kept inside her self-recriminating mind. I'm nearly certain my parents felt they failed Melanie in every way, and they mourned and regretted the loss of her and the way things had gone. I think Melanie felt some kind of failure there too. I think our whole family felt failure, because we loved each other but we couldn't pull it together to show it, at least not all at once.

I don't know all the things that drove my mom from deep inside her, but I am pretty sure she was a little girl who was taught to stay quiet, and small, and learned to despise those who craved drama as a way of life from her mother, who was always sick and needy and overly dramatic. My mom valued independence but sought love and acceptance, things I think she sometimes felt she didn't get from us. Had I asked the right questions of my mother when she was living, I might have learned her mother was smothering and judgmental. In turn, my mother was a worrier, but she didn't smother; she was anxious, but rarely showed it. She could be judgmental, but only in her worst moments, when her mind was leaving her, and I can't blame her for that. My mother was the very best for me she could be, and I love her for it. She comes to me now in random pennies on the ground and red birds in the sky. So for every penny I see on the ground, for every cardinal and scarlet tanager that crosses my path, I thank my mother for her hello. For every beautiful goal in my life I reach after years and years of trying, I thank my mother for helping me get to it. She talks to God and the Universe, I'm sure. She nudges them to see me through things.

Just like my parents, my sisters and I have weaknesses of our own. Some of them lie very close to the surface. Melanie is self-centered and selfish and short-tempered, without empathy, cold and defensive. Grace is weak, incapable, afraid, anxious, and needy. I am reckless, thoughtless, irresponsible, flighty, and unreliable. But underneath our thin skins are thick veins full of the reasons for what we are. They started close to the surface where they first came in from the outside, when we were small; those experiences like pinpricks that sometimes broke through to the vein on the first try. Other times it took repeated pain, repeated pokes to change us, to get to the vein, to commit the tainted blood coursing deep into us for a lifetime, never to reach the surface again, like those jelly-looking animals that live in the bottom of the ocean, clear and unseeing.

Still, God and the Universe want the same things for all of us—to be happy, to find peace, to live the lives we are meant to lead. Sometimes that requires nudging; sometimes it requires slaps across the face. There was a point in my life I thought how lucky I was that nothing really bad ever happened to me. At other times I have felt bravado for how strong I've become, how much I can take, how easily I find a way around or through the difficulties. There were times in the past I cried for the fear of knowing that at some point

I would have to deal with an end, or deal with a loss and I thought I couldn't bear it. I was anxious; I created in my mind all the worst endings before they even happened. For each of those moments I have learned there will be a counter-moment, the second when you are given the grace to learn you will survive, or you won't have to endure, because it has happened, already, just like that.

I never wanted to have children. Now I have a child, an 81-year-old toddler who needs me. A kid at the very age I always said I wouldn't want one, because they talk nonsensically and you can't understand anything they say. A toddler would be the hardest, I thought, because you can't escape their needs; they are not old enough to care for themselves so you are stuck, trapped, like a prisoner in shackles, having to monitor them and wash them and feed them. They are attached to your hip. I have that situation now, in my life, the one I never wanted. This is fate, in my life. It's not so bad after all.

I used to dream about losing Cerin: in the woods, on a trail, to a car that doesn't see him as he runs along the edge of the road. He ran off many times during our years together; he was the dog who always knew where he was, even if I didn't, and after a while I didn't worry about him anymore. I knew he would find his way back to the trailhead when he was ready. I hated waiting for him because I hate to wait for anyone, another personal flaw of mine. Now I wait an undetermined amount of time for my father to pass, for my life to change again, for me to have the freedom I think I need to be happy. I learned to appreciate Cerin's drive to have what he wanted—and to take a brash step to grasp it whenever the moment struck him without concern for where it might lead. I liked to think he was like me, in some ways, I suppose. Rushing off to Arizona without much thought, leaving behind people who cared about me, and jobs that supported me, for simply my own adventure. Cerin and I found adventure together. I could understand where he was coming from when he ran off, when he stopped to dig furiously, living in the moment, tiring his body, filling his muzzle with mud and yet still digging, sniffing, in search of what he wasn't sure, but it was there, so close.

When Cerin got sick I had moved back to Arizona just for a short stay during one of the most confused and unsteady adventures of my life. In early November of 2008 I had moved back to Michigan for good to be close to my family. But I had left behind a boy, Kevin, who needed me, I thought, and so I ventured back for a few short weeks to figure out whether we could make it work forever, or not. A life with this boy, Kevin, would have been completely wrong, and so far off the path that God and the Universe had in store for me, I could barely see it anymore. But I struggled to figure out what to do anyway. I wouldn't listen to my intuition or my heart. I was torn— and so in my worst moment I took on the characteristics of me and my family. I was afraid, anxious, self-defeating; I was defensive and irresponsible. So in late December 2008 I drove back to Arizona for the sixth time with a sick Cerin in the back seat. Cerin had started to show signs of illness when I was still back in Ann Arbor, so I had taken him to a vet there. But they hadn't been able to determine what was wrong with him. They thought it might be congestive heart failure. Somehow I knew it wasn't. I didn't know what it was, but it wasn't that.

Cerin was stoic and made it through the trip, but within two weeks of arriving in Arizona, it was clear he was dying. I took him to his vet in Arizona, Dr. Chris, who knew Cerin well and had seen us through many years of loving care. I told Dr. Chris I wanted Cerin to stay overnight, hoping they could track down the cause of his not eating and get to the bottom of what was wrong. I had taken the first job I could find when I got back to Arizona, and it was a seventy-mile commute, so leaving Cerin with them made the most sense. I left Cerin with Dr. Chris on a Monday and on Tuesday I drove home from work. It was dark; I was talking to my friend Suma, my sage friend whose words had helped me get through all kinds of adventures, bad and good. I called Suma on my way home from work Tuesday night. While we were talking on my commute home, I found myself in the vet's parking lot. I thought I would say hello to Cerin, scratch his long nose and let him know I was here, waiting for him to get better. I parked and glanced at the clock in my car realizing how late it was. I would come back tomorrow. I backed out of the parking lot and drove home.

Wednesday morning while I was in a meeting, Dr. Chris called four times. When I saw my messages, I went outside to the picnic tables to call back. The vet was in tears; while they were examining him that morning Cerin had gone into cardiac arrest and died. All I could think was that I had missed my chance to see him. We cried together, Dr. Chris and me. He asked if I wanted to see Cerin one more time before they sent him for cremation. I was seventy miles away, standing on the back patio staring out into the desert of East Sedona.

"No," I said, "I want to remember him the way I saw him last."

"I understand," the vet said.

I hung up, and wailed. I had never cried like that before. I've never cried like that since. My wailing was for Cerin, for me and for things to come; things I didn't know yet. Two years later my dad would have his stroke and I would hardly cry for the loss of the father I knew him to be. By then I think my heavy heart of badness had grown heavier. And after all, I still had my dad with me, one way or the other. Cerin had been taken away in an instant, forever. By the time my mom died, my heart had been broken for so long--pulled so far down into a place I never thought it would emerge from--that I didn't cry much for her either, at least not at first. Maybe that's because her demise came systematically, with enough time to process but not enough time to dwell. I would cry later for Mom, at times I least expected, over things that seemed unrelated. I cried for all the losses that seemed to pile up as time went by.

I mostly look back at all of this as a blessing. A random, unrequested blessing that turned out to be the way I learned to see I wasn't just all those things my thin skin has lying just below the surface.

We all have beautiful memories and pieces of life that are a part of us. We all have good, and bad, and something in-between. Of all my beautiful memories and crazy life experiences, I really have only two regrets: first, I didn't get out of the car at the vet's office and go inside to scratch Cerin's nose one last time, because it was a moment in my lifetime I missed. It was one last chance to show him how much I loved him. It was one solitary remaining opportunity lost, forever. My other regret is exactly the same, but for my mom. I didn't say goodbye to her while she still breathed her last hours on the planet, no matter how far she was at that moment from the person I knew her to be.

I don't yet know what the last moments of any life must be like. But in those last hours or minutes or seconds there must be any number of things the dying want more than anything else to feel, to taste, to live over again. My final acts of kindness during these two events on my life path—the deaths of Cerin and my mom-- were not my proudest moments. They are moments I cannot change, but they are lessons I take with me. I will face something like this again; I will see other people I know facing these things. I will have advice. I don't follow the self-defeating me down this path anymore. I take a lighter heart. I let the heaviness lift a little. I think it is okay. I think Cerin and my mom, the dad I had before and the one I have now, my sisters—both of them, and every other little thing I carry from the forty acres would want it that way.

CPSIA information can be obtained at www.ICGtesting.com
Printed in the USA
BVOW06s0224170715

408918BV00009B/206/P